CW01261696

UNKNOWN LEWES

UNKNOWN LEWES

An Historical Geography

by

John Houghton

Tartarus Press

UNKNOWN LEWES, AN HISTORICAL GEOGRAPHY
by John Houghton, was first published
by the Tartarus Press, 1997, at
5 Birch Terrace, Hangingbirch Lane,
Horam, East Sussex, TN21 OPA.
Copyright © John Houghton, 1997
ISBN 1 872621 28 7
Second edition, 1998
Printed in Great Britain by Antony Rowe Ltd,
Chippenham, Wiltshire.

CONTENTS

Introduction	v
Acknowledgements	viii
Chapter 1. Ways In	1
Chapter 2. The Threat Dictates the Shape	18
Chapter 3. Defence	38
Chapter 4. The Management of the Town	50
Chapter 5. Church and Parish	83
Chapter 6. The Market	106
Chapter 7. Westout and Without	118
Chapter 8. The Suburb of Southover	137
Chapter 9. Conclusion	154
Notes	160
Appendices	171

Panorama of Lewes from the Mount in St John's churchyard. Lambert, 1778.

Introduction

Any title is bound to be pretentious. One of the things that stopped me for years from writing about Lewes was finding a title. *A History of Lewes* would not do. This is not a history, but a shot at bringing together bits of history so that the whole is greater than the parts.

Archaeology can involve excavation to destruction, but writing about the past is usually a harmless activity. One does not destroy the evidence, even if one misunderstands it. Someone better can come along, and do a re-write. No harm is done, except perhaps to one's reputation. If what I have written provokes someone to a considered counter-attack, then it serves a useful purpose. I claim no reputation, so I have nothing to lose.

Some previous writers avoided things because they didn't fit, or they were inconvenient or contradicted dearly held beliefs. Some have avoided difficult aspects because there is no primary evidence to support their study. The title *Unknown Lewes* is as misleading and pretentious as most others, although perhaps not quite so much as *A History of Lewes*. Some previous writers have done marvellous work, but got it wrong. If they had not, later workers like me might not have spotted their mistakes and had the opportunity to put them right. We might not have considered the matters at all.

Sometimes a thing looks wrong, and provokes fresh study. Without mistakes in the past, we might not have the opportunity to deal with them, right or wrong. Among many previous writers on Lewes, three persons stand out and should be mentioned. Paul Dunvan was the bashful author of William Lee's 1795 publication, the *History of Lewes and Brighthelmstone*. He was French, or of French extraction, and was for many years usher at Lewes Grammar School. He certainly had access to the town books, and to many original manuscripts, some of which may no longer be available. As a contemporary of Thomas Woolgar, he may have had access to Woolgar's own careful collection of manuscript notes. Dunvan's history is a very readable, pioneering work, full of interest and contemporary comment. It is also liberally larded with purple passages of prejudice and intolerance, but all the more fun to read as a result.

Thomas Walker Horsfield (d.1837) followed Dunvan thirty years later. An historian and minister of the Westgate Chapel (then and now Unitarian), he wrote a two volume *History and Antiquities of Lewes and Vicinity* which was published by Baxter in 1824. His work is a great store of knowledge.

Walter Godfrey, architect and historian, lived his hobby dangerously. As a writer and lecturer he had a prodigious and high quality output, a great deal of which remains unpublished. With such an output he was bound to make a few mistakes, but these must never be allowed to detract from his principal achievement of getting so many things right. It would be a foolish worker who did not check first to see what Walter Godfrey had said or done.

Even so, historical documents, the remaining buildings and the layout of the town are the true witnesses to the past, so it is to these that I look for our story. If history is about chaps, and geography is about maps, then I may concentrate too much on maps and not chaps, but that is the way the evidence forces me to go. As W. G. Hoskins says:

> *We may study with our guide books all the historic, individual features of a town and get to know them. But then - if we are taking our time and stay to look at the town as a whole, walk around it in the cool and quiet of the evening when the shops are shut, and the traffic has gone home, we can really see its contours and its bone*

INTRODUCTION

structure - other questions begin to arise in the mind, which even the best of guide books does not answer. Why is the town just like this, this shape, this plan, this size? Why do its streets run this particular way and not in some other way that seems more logical to us? ... in short, what gives the town this particular landscape?[1]

Here then is my view of the past of this lovely town. I have learnt much in the process of study. I have taken care to see that matters are accurate, but I have not hesitated to deal with the unknown, the non-conforming, the awkward and the inconvenient fact, and I have indulged in quite a lot of guesswork. If in the event my conclusions are wrong it will not have been for want of trying.

Volume 134 of the *Sussex Archaeological Collections* appeared just as I was getting to the end of this work. Of the Grey Friars, I had written (over the course of time) from 'nothing is known' through to 'it would be unwise to anticipate the report' of the archaeological investigations. Of the Castle, John Farrant's report makes my work on the Castle something of a duplication. I live in fear that some new discovery or publication may prove me wrong even before this ink is dry. If this is so, then so be it. Meanwhile, come and walk round the town, as Hoskins suggests.

I would like to pay tribute to all the help I have received from many people, but particularly from John Farrant, 'Ben' Franklin and Christopher Whittick, all of whom will be amused to see that I have ignored all their suggestions, helpful though they were. The end result, success or failure, is mine alone.

Acknowledgements

The author would like to thank the following for their permission to use copyright illustrations and maps in the text:

Sussex Archaeological Society (frontispiece, 4.1, 4.3, 5.3, 5.6, 5.9, 5.11, 7.1, 7.2, 8.2); *Lewes Civic Society* (2.2, 5.8, 5.10, 8.3); *East Sussex Record Office* (4.2); *Ordnance Survey* (5.4, 5.5). The plan of Castle Acre Priory (8.4) is by courtesy of English Heritage Photo Library, London.

Chapter One
Ways In

Many people who live in or visit Lewes, the attractive county town of East Sussex, enjoy the beauties it offers. These, though satisfying enough in themselves, would be even more enjoyable if the evolution of the town could be more easily understood. To understand Lewes, one has to go back to the time before the town was there, to see how it started, and why. Places happen where people meet. Towns are not created in some kind of a vacuum. They grow up where people meet, to exchange the time of day, or goods, news and occasionally blows. Some landmark or particular feature may give a name to the meeting place, even though this feature may have since disappeared. The name of the town may recall some event or characteristic, now lost in the mists of time. Lewes started as a place where people met as they moved along the roads and trackways of the area.

The oldest European road began somewhere in the central part of the continent. The grazing herds and the people that followed them wandered north and west as the ice cap retreated at the end of the last glaciation, passing over the land bridge between France and England, the area now covered by the English Channel. Much modified since then, the road is now a modern confection, since in places new objectives grew up to deflect the older path. Even so, the South Downs Way (as it is in this region now called) avoided Lewes, though it has since warped in the direction of the town. If you stand on Ditchling Beacon and look towards Firle Beacon, the lie of the land takes you along the chalk ridge by Falmer, through which the railway now tunnels. This is the watershed between Lewes and Brighton, and the way to go. The true line then climbs to

Kingston Hill and continues as the old ridgeway above Kingston to cross the River Ouse well below Lewes itself.

Of the roads the Romans constructed, one ran from beyond Chichester to Brighton. The eastward continuation of this went on over Newmarket and Kingston Hills to Southover, now known as Juggs Road. At Southover, a branch now called Rotten Row diverts directly to the site of the West Gate of Lewes. There it is joined by a road which leads from the South Downs Way, by way of Ashcombe, to the western edge of Lewes. These roads aimed for the ford over the river, now served by Lewes Bridge. This does not yet prove the existence of the town but it does argue a need to cross the river. This need was caused by another Roman road, the second century 'London to Lewes' route. Its rather misleading name gives a fictitious sense of the importance of Lewes at this time, for the town had yet even to come into existence. It is really the 'Malling Down to London' road, and a branch road from Malling Down followed the current line of Church Lane, Malling to the riverside at Old Malling, the earliest recorded site of occupation in the area east of the river, and so far as is known the earliest occupation site in the environs of Lewes. The monastery at Old Malling was founded in the mid-eighth century AD, and by AD 838 the Church in Canterbury established or re-established its claim on it. With a road from Canterbury to Malling and various parishes that needed to be visited right across Sussex to the very western edge of Chichester, the influence of Canterbury came to alter the emphasis from the Downland ridgeways to the river crossings. The river too is a way into Lewes. It is the way early Saxon settlers came, and it was they who created the town. As they colonised northwards, so their road lifts up from the river level, making for Offham to the north, and then swinging west along the foot of the Downs, to Allington and beyond to Ditchling, and continuing north to Barcombe and Chailey.

In looking for origins we must consider hundreds,

manors and parishes, the pre-cursors of our local administration. The hundred has been the longest surviving administrative unit in England. Modern District and County Councils are mere parvenus compared with the at least 900 years in the life of the hundreds. Hundreds originated as groups of one hundred families, and can be traced back to the late fifth century AD. By the tenth century they had become areas of land defined by boundaries[1]. An enquiry of 1274-5, shows that Lewes was not part of any hundred. The earliest maps to depict hundred boundaries show that the old borough of Lewes was independent of the hundred system. Figure 1.1 shows a detail from Richard Budgen's map of 1724 (to make it easier to read, I have suppressed some symbols irrelevant at this stage). At that time Lewes was bounded on the north by Barcombe Hundred, west and south by Swanborough Hundred, and by a bulge in the south which appears to be Southover. Hundred boundaries when eventually drawn would have recognised existing territorial arrangements, so we have to assume that when it was thought a good idea to set them up, Lewes already had a separate identity and was not included in the system. The surrounding hundreds simply wrapped around it. Modern Hamsey parish, part of the hundred of Barcombe, now divides the Lewes parish of St John into 'sub Castro' and 'Without'. St John sub Castro is within the town. St John Without (i.e. outside the town) is in the hundred of Barcombe. This is some later arrangement, for originally the parish of St John must have extended for many miles outside Lewes to the north, as St John Without still does. The Westout parishes of Lewes are also outside the original town boundary, in Swanborough Hundred. Now, when we look at modern Lewes, we can see that it has expanded so that parts of it are in Barcombe or Swanborough Hundreds.

Danish (or Viking) raids along the coast of Sussex started about AD 790, and got progressively worse over the next hundred years. Alfred became King of Wessex in AD 871, but

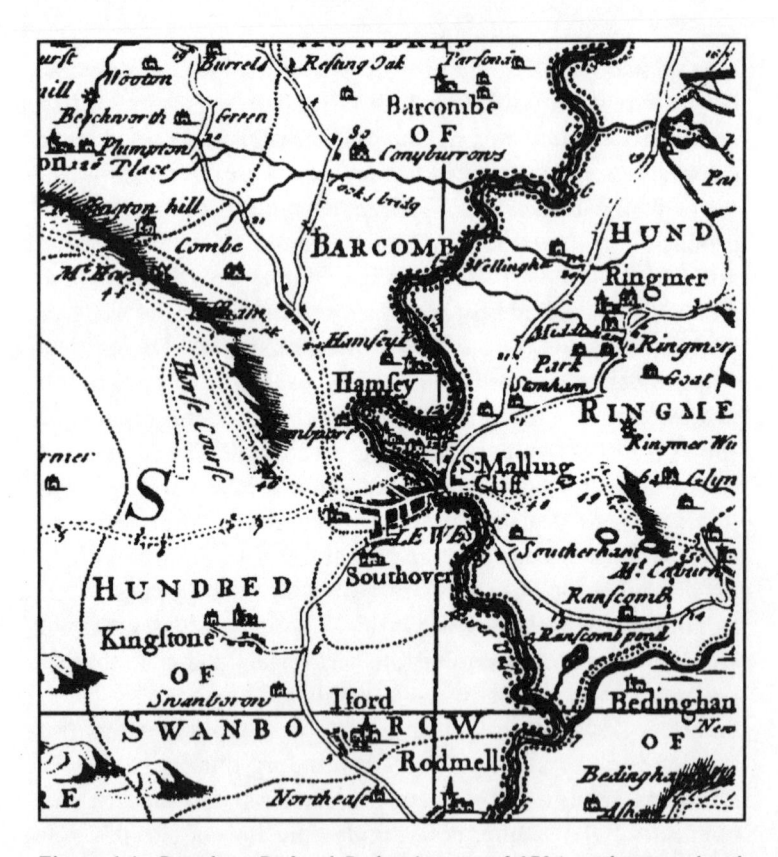

Figure 1.1. *Based on Richard Budgen's map of 1724, with some detail removed.*

earlier, his elder brother King Aethelred had called a meeting of the wise men, the *Witanagemot*. They discussed what could be done about the raiding which so troubled the kingdom. Many years later, Alfred's will recalled the meeting, and that it took place at 'Swinbeorgum'. Place name experts have suggested that this is unlikely to indicate Swanborough. However, it could have been a simple spelling mistake or a faulty recollection. It happens now, it could easily have happened then.

WAYS IN

The Saxon kings had land in the area called the manor of Niworde, which covered most of Swanborough Hundred. Edward the Confessor's widow, Queen Edith, still held Niworde as a royal manor in 1066. In the manor, one and a half miles outside Lewes, lies the present day village of Kingston. Perhaps here lies the true origin of Lewes. *'The Kingston, managed for him* [the king] *by a Reeve, was a fundamental unit in Old English organisation of justice and finance. To it the tillers of the soil would deliver the produce which made up the monarch's food rent'* and *'In the Kingston, a royal estate provided with a jail and managed by the King's reeve, we find the precursor of the Hundred Court.'* [2] The name 'Kingston' would have lapsed when Lewes was created to take over the functions of the former estate, and the name of the manor, 'Niworde' (new enclosure), probably originated then. Among the locals it would not have been so easy to get rid of the older name and Kingston it remained, to surface again in the eleventh century, when Niworde was divided up with one part becoming the manor of Kingston.

Alfred may have been struck by the similarity between the site of Lewes and that of his capital, Winchester. A river running down each valley, crossing points at the high tide limit, and long fingers of Downland pointing eastwards into the flood plain all sustain the similarity. The early defensive camps of Mount Caburn east of Lewes, and St Katherine's Hill east of Winchester, both flank the river, pinching the high tide crossing points. Both towns were protected by water on several sides, and were particularly strongly defended against possible attack from the east, the main direction of 'Danish' threat. It may have been the lessons learned from battles in AD 871 and AD 878, when Alfred saw how the Danish invaders created fortified strong points, that led him to plan his own series of forts of which Lewes was one. Perhaps a memory of his bother's Witan would have reminded Alfred that the site would be a good one. Certainly, if you want to experience the quality of the site of Lewes as a defensive, 'gap' town, Swanborough Hill offers as good a viewing point as any.

The later manors of Iford, Swanborough, Kingston, and the lands that were to become the manor of Southover, must all once have been part of the royal manor of Niworde. When the Norman lord of Lewes, William de Warenne, created those new manors he took in the separate, already established, but small manors of Ashcombe and Winterbourne to the north of Niworde, which together closed off the land available to an expanding Lewes on its westward side. This is why Westout, although mainly in the borough of Lewes, remained outside the earliest town boundaries, within Swanborough Hundred. A hundred or a manor constitutes a right and a responsibility over land, these are not easy to map.

Appendix A lists the manors which held land in Lewes in 1086, at the time of the Domesday survey. It also indicates, as far as possible, how many plots of land each manor owned. According to Domesday, in 1066 King Edward had 127 properties in Lewes. But when you count them up individually they total 113. So Domesday contradicts itself, and only 113 can be seen, so either 113 must be correct, or fourteen have been overlooked. The de Warennes later took into their own hands many of the smaller manors in the rape, so any hope of correcting this confusion seems to be lost. We can be sure that land in Lewes would be owned by the great magnates by freehold of outside manors, or free or copyhold of the borough. There is plenty of scope here for confusion. The pattern of ownership at Domesday is shown in Figure 1.2.

Virtually no pre-Conquest historical evidence survives for Lewes. We can only consider what historians of quality and standing have had to say about late Anglo-Saxon towns in general, and apply it by analogy to Lewes.[3] The main functions and institutions which towns of the period supported have had a continuing, shaping effect on Lewes. These were defence, law and order, the courts, administration, market,

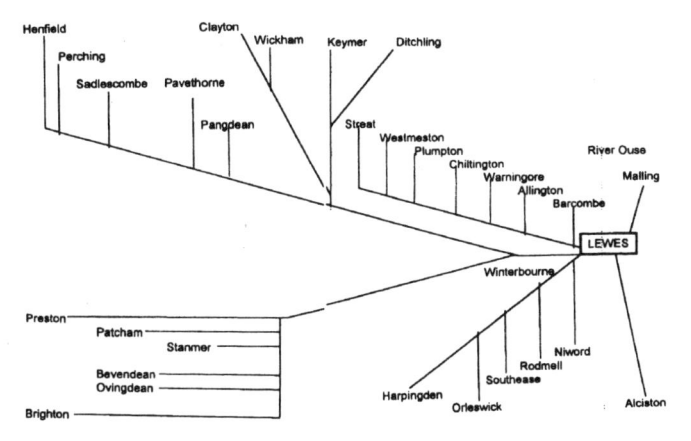

Figure 1.2. Domesday tenants holding lands in Lewes Rape with Burgages in Lewes. (There is no significance in the groupings above, which are used only to keep each manor in a relative position to geographically.)

mint and money, and the Church. Despite their tendency to coalesce or cross-over each other's boundaries, I shall try to maintain these definitions wherever possible.

Documentary evidence of the local administration that had evolved before the Conquest refers to 'burgesses' holding the land of the king within Lewes. Each plot of land within the town had a house. A burgess lived in a house, on a plot. Nowadays historians used the term 'burgage' to describe houses on plots, and burgage tenure as the way in which they were owned.

Burgesses who did not hold land of the king were reckoned as 'lying in' or annexed to the manor to which they were tied. Manors as far away as Patcham had burgesses in Lewes. Some manors with interests in the town did not have burgesses at all. Already, if there was once some logic to the pattern of land tenure, it had begun to be eroded well before the Conquest. For these reasons the 'burh', the Anglo-Saxon name for a defensible town such as Lewes, was already different from the more common manor or village. The inhabitants dwelt in one place in law, their parent manor, but another place in fact, in the burh. The earliest meaning of burh is 'stronghold'. It is a fastness, and a place of some special importance. In the oldest laws written a man's house is described as a burh. This may imply that the houses referred to had a palisade or an entrenchment surrounding them. The king's burh was particularly protected by its enjoyment of the king's special peace. The king's special peace was better than anyone else's. *'In the King's borough is the King's house, for his house peace prevails in the streets.'* [4] In a royal burh, crime was countered by special punishment, enshrined in law. Penalties for those who broke the peace were greater within than without. Evidence from elsewhere suggests that a crime in a royal burh was regarded as crime against the king. So long as the king had burgesses in Lewes it was claimed as a royal burh. The king's special peace defined the limits of the burh, irrespective of any physical perimeter created by walls and gates. In some places the king's special peace extended for three miles, three furlongs and three feet from his house or houses. In one example it was even more precise, being three miles, three furlongs, three acre breadths, nine feet, nine hand breadths and nine barleycorns.[5] Short of getting on your knees and doing some careful measurement, this must have made it difficult to know whether you were inside the king's peace or not. In Lewes a circle drawn from the West Gate of three miles radius takes one to the outer edges of the parishes of St Ann Without, St John Without and Rodmell, to include chapels at Smithwick, Allington and Northease respectively. I believe this is the first time it has been suggested that such an arrangement may have existed, and it will be further explored in Chapter Five.

By the tenth century, the scope of the burh was evolving. According to the laws of King Alfred's grandson Athelstan, each burh must have a moot and a mint. A moot is a meeting, essentially acting as a court of the town. By Athelstan's time,

Lewes had a mint. There is no record of a moot, but if it had the one it surely had the other. The moot would have been held three times each year, and was a very necessary part of the town's administration. The burgesses, in matters affecting the concerns of the burh, needed some central control, as they were otherwise subject only to their respective hundred or manor court. We shall see this need again reflected in the courts held in the town during the sixteenth century, but for now it is enough to claim that, with many burgesses dependent upon outside manors, a court there had to be. This illustrates another difference between a burh and a village. The burh had its own court, whilst the village was subject to a hundred or manor court, which might have jurisdiction over more than one village.

During the peril of Danish raiding, entering the burh would have conferred a blessing. In a fortified burh there would be a cluster of inhabited dwellings, defended by a surrounding earthwork, enjoying the added protection of the king's special peace. Lewes appears near the top of the lists of towns chosen to be burhs. It was to be more than just a refuge in troubled times. It was to share with Chichester, and perhaps with Hastings, the major burden of the defence of Sussex. It had wide lands which it was its responsibility to defend and it is likely that all the land between the rivers Ouse and Adur, the early rape of Lewes, was its territory. The land was to be burdened with burh maintenance, and so far as can be certain, the rape maintains its burh.

The Domesday Book is more forthcoming about other towns than it is about Lewes. In Oxford, for example, the king had twenty 'mural houses' and others were held by other lords. Their tenure required that *'If there be need and the King gives order, they shall repair the Wall'*.[6] In Chester, in order to repair the wall the reeve called out one man from every hide in the county. These arrangements must surely predate Domesday and therefore originated before the Norman

Conquest. The burgess was originally a professional warrior. He was placed in the burh by the lord of his manor, who probably provided his weapons and his subsistence. A warrior's heirs had a general obligation to return the weapons with which he had been provided, to whichever manor he belonged, and this was known as 'heriot'. Land in Lewes, irrespective of the manor to which it belonged, was free of heriot and this is a solid bit of evidence for the early Anglo-Saxon origins of the town. Heriot later became a cash payment or the provision of some valuable in kind. In Lewes the concession was that no heriot was payable, whichever manor owned the property. Defence of the burh was thus an hereditary obligation resting on the heir's manor, and the heir would take over the arms and armour as his heritage, with the benefits and obligations that went with them. The fact that no heriot was payable to Lewes must represent a concession from the earliest days.

The formal moot court (sometimes called '*Burh*gemot' or '*Burh*witan') was needed to organise the important tasks of the administration of the burh and to perform judicial functions. There was also a need to promote close bonds and a sense of unity. As the burgesses came from different districts and owed allegiance to different lords, this was done also by the creation of 'brotherhoods' or *Cniht-gilds* (knight gilds), gilds of brothers-in-arms or some other communal activity. From one of these grew the merchant gilds, and Lewes certainly had a merchant gild by the second half of the eleventh century.

The pre-Conquest burh had also become a formalised centre of trade. It had a market, and for the better protection of traders it had a licensed moneyer to mint coins which could be trusted as authentic. This process had its roots in the special peace of the burh. Inside the burh people could meet to buy and sell in relative safety, enjoying a trading base more secure than any to be found outside. It offered a means of establishing the validity of their trading by way of the testimony of their peers, and the trustworthy coinage was safe to use as a store of value.

In addition to providing food for the burgesses and paying the king's food rents, manorial surpluses could also be supplied for general sale or barter. Perhaps burgesses traded on behalf of their manor. At a later stage, laws directed against theft required that men should only buy and sell in appointed markets and not elsewhere. Traders began to build booths in the burh, and so a market place evolved. Laws were developed which prohibited trade outside the market, ordering that all transactions were to be attested by trustworthy men. So the market was not a nebulous phenomenon, it was something established by law. Twelve official witnesses were appointed for the smaller burhs, of which Lewes was one. Here again we can see the origins of the later town government, the Society of Twelve of the sixteenth century, along with the clerks of the market and other officers of the borough. Those who enjoyed the validation of the market had to pay for the privilege. The proceeds of rents, tolls and the fines of the borough courts went to the king, who shared part (the 'third penny') with the earl. 'Toll' was part of the Domesday issues of the burh of Lewes, and came from a market of long standing. With relative peace from about AD 950 on, the warlike functions of the burgesses became redundant. Lords of outside manors kept their burgesses only when it suited them. It could advantage a lord to decrease his land holdings in the burh by selling his property and transferring with it the defence obligations to someone else. It was a characteristic of property in a burh, and Lewes was no exception, that land could be freely bought, sold, exchanged, divided up or added to without the need for any royal consent, unlike other lands. Perhaps a small tradesman or merchant would take on the defence burden as he took on a property in the town for a consideration, gambling that the obligation would not be called on, or that he could buy his way out of it. At Chester any hide which did not send a man when called on had to pay a fine of two pounds. The equivalent at Lewes was *'if the King wished to send his men in his absence to guard the sea, they collect 20s from all men whosoever the land was, and those who had charge of arms in the ships had these shillings'*.[7] This emphasises that defence was a duty of all landowners in the town. It may also indicate that because of Lewes's closeness to the sea, its defence obligation covered ships, not armies.

Even by Domesday, the earliest origins of the ancient boroughs would have become obscure. How much more so for us 900 years after Domesday and 1,100 years after Alfred sat looking down from Swanborough Hill. The land on which the burgess properties were laid out came from a common owner; the king. He allocated plots of land in the town to the lords of the surrounding manors, and imposed the obligation on them of organising the town's defences, and then defending it.

The burgess plots were a standard size, held of a fixed, and even by the time we can first see it, a rather nominal rent. This rent later became no more than an acknowledgement of fealty, the duty of the man to his lord, a 'quit-rent' known in the Domesday Book as 'gable'. Apart from fealty (which included the defence obligation) and attendance at the king's courts, the holder of land within the town was 'quit' of all other exactions, including, as we have seen, from heriot. However obscure the eventual quit-rents may have become, the obligations were clear. In 1268-9, Richard de Playz, an important landowner, died, and in the inquisition on his death it was stated that *'he held ... of the Earl de Warenne by what service they do not know except that the aforesaid tenements owe suit at Sussex County Court from month to month and at the Earle of Warennnes court at Lewes from three weeks to three weeks'.* [8] The eventual land owners were diffuse, but their ownership sprang from a common origin, a common obligation and a standard pattern. In 1237 a conveyance is *'... free and quit of all secular demands saving the service of the Earl Warenne namely 6d ... ',*[9] and as late as 1816 a property was let for seven years and the tenant agreed to pay *'... land tax and Lord's quit rent'*.[10] Although in later years quit-rents seldom figure in conveyances, they were carefully recorded in the borough rentals, whether they could actually be collected or not. So there is the pattern, however shadowy, of the elements that define a burh in general, and Lewes in particular.

One possible survival of the earliest town administration is in a way the most convincing. The purpose of a burh was to provide a refuge for the surrounding country people to flee to in times of attack. Their houses were mere sticks and straw, their crops expendable, and it was their families and cattle which represented their capital. In Lewes, until the end of the eighteenth century, all land in the northern part of the town (from Market Lane to the end of North Street) was clear of buildings. Archaeologists say that there is little evidence of any medieval occupation here other than for itinerant camping.[11] This was the space into which the country people could flee for refuge. In AD 892, the Anglo-Saxon Chronicle recorded the capture by Danish raiders of a small fort in the marshes of what is now the eastern Rother. It was only half-built and was defended by a few peasants.[12] That fort was only a quarter or a fifth of the size of Lewes or Chichester, both of which were fortified towns, and not just forts. When that little fort in the marshes fell to the Danish raiders, Lewes was sufficiently strong to have resisted any attack. Looking at the places listed as burhs, it seems that tenth-century Sussex was divided into blocks, each with a fortress so that no settlement was more than forty, and in some cases not more than thirty miles from its nearest place of defence and refuge. So as early as twenty years after King Alfred's death, Lewes was established and flourishing as a defended market town.

All this raises the problem of the origin of the name. Tantalising early references (in immediately post-Conquest documents referring to about AD 961) refer to 'Hamme with

Laewe' or 'Hamme juxta Laewes', suggesting but not explaining a connection between Lewes and Hamsey.[13] Early tenth-century Lewes had two moneyers, and what the coins can tell us is interesting. The earliest known coins read 'Lae Urb', and thereafter follow a variety of spellings, of which *Laehwge, Laewea, Laewwe, Leawe* all try to tell us something.[14] Richard Coates justifies the variant spellings as a scribe's attempts to render in Latin an Anglo-Saxon word, and that they really do try to sound like 'Hlaewes'.[15] He points to the old pronunciation, 'Looze', which certainly was still being used locally within the last fifty years, but claims that two syllables would have been correct in the Middle English period.[16] 'Looze' is the pronunciation still used for the Old Rectory House, known as 'The Lewes' in the parish of Walton, Norfolk, held at one time by Lewes Priory.[17] However, more recently Coates has modified his view and leans in favour of the name being a rare survival from Celtic (Brittonic),[18] and in the absence of any known settlement at Lewes before Anglo-Saxon times, the name may be a regional one (*'for the South Downs in general, or the Ouse/Adur block of Downland in particular'*),[19] or derived perhaps from the name of a tribe inhabiting the region.

The *Burghal Hidage*, a document of the tenth century, tells us about Anglo-Saxon burhs and covers Lewes in its descriptions. Each hide of land had to send one man to build a defence and defend the town. One must not read too much into this, for as Stenton pointed out *'... the organisation which it records was brought into being for the sole purpose of providing garrisons for the fortresses. It gives no ground for any theory that the districts assigned to fortresses were used as administrative as well as military units'.*[20]

The *Burghal Hidage* has been the subject of much study, in particular by D. Hill.[21] He shows that there are seven versions of an original lost text to choose from, one of which assigned 1,300 hides of land to Lewes which it had to defend, and from which to draw a garrison for defence. An earlier version assigned only 1,200, which may be a mistake or may suggest that there was a later increase of the assessment. The Domesday Book lists only 674 hides and a handful of fractions, which is at first sight inconvenient. There is an academic argument for a 'small' hide and a 'large' hide in the *Burghal Hidage*. The ninth century 1,300 hides, if calculated as small hides, would rate 650 large hides, so 674 could be about right. It is a guess, but it does enable us to make some progress. The lands in the rape of Lewes had by 1086 been so chopped about, with bits on both sides assigned to the flanking rapes, that we shall never know the truth. The fractions are interesting, since by Domesday the hide still seems to retain a part of its original purpose in defining an area of land which could support a family. Good land would support a family more easily than poor, so a hide could be bigger or smaller, according to its quality. Sometimes there is a difference between actual hides and taxed hides. The full argument is set out in detail in an appendix to Morris's Domesday Book.[22]

Before leaving the evidence for early Lewes, Southover (now part of the Lewes Borough) is a lower spur of land south of Lewes, separated from the early town by the Winterbourne stream, truly winter bourne as it flows only in the winter months. Although the name is used in documents of the eleventh century it doesn't appear in the Domesday Book. It had to belong somewhere else under or inside some other grouping or heading. The Southover peninsula, protected by water on three sides, once carried a through-route sufficiently important to justify a timber-built wayside chapel beside the track along the ridge to and from a river crossing at Southerham. At its western end the parish boundary used to cross the line of the Romanised trackway from Brighton, near an Edwardian house called Saxonbury. The name records the finding here of a sixth-seventh century, and thus pagan, Anglo-Saxon burial ground containing at least thirty-two inhumation burials.[23] This is the earliest known burial ground close to Lewes, although there is another across the river on Malling Hill. The cemetery at Saxonbury was a settlement cemetery, not a warriors' burial ground. The absence of Christian burials, if known practice from elsewhere holds good, suggests that the settlement from which these people came was situated some distance away from where they were buried. It is possible that the Saxonbury cemetery may not relate to Southover at all, but to nearby Winterbourne, described as a 'famous place' (for whatever reason) in an AD 966 document.[24] Even so, the low peninsula of Southover was not deserted before the Normans came. The Ouse, Winterbourne and Cockshut rivers formed water boundaries on three sides and Priory charters call the land on which the Priory was built 'The Island'.[25]

This must be enough (although so much more could be speculated) of the earliest days, when Lewes was beginning to take shape. A land crossed by several trackways, some perhaps even earlier than man, two of which made for a river crossing at the high tide level, and others which joined one or other of them to march together to that same fording point. The Saxonbury burial ground beside one of these roads points probably to an earlier settlement. All of this was on a royal manor, a Kingston, a local centre for law, order, and the collection of the monarch's food rents. The series of damaging raids by Danish 'pirates' caused the laying out of defensive points, one of which was to become Lewes. The higher finger of Downland became the site on which a defended town was planted. The site was defended not just for itself, but as a place of refuge for the surrounding area, mainly west of the river boundary. As the settlement grew, the local tracks and ridgeways diverted so as to recognise the new place where people met, where they could exchange, physically or intellectually. The travellers journeyed, crossed, and built new meeting places. The human needs of law, order, Church, administration, market, money and mint were introduced, so by the early tenth century a flourishing town had been created, a centre for defence, but more than that, a centre for those other functions without which a place was not a burh. Hopefully, enough background has been painted in to allow us to look more closely at the internal details. We can climb the hill and look in.

Chapter Two
The Threat Dictates the Shape

There was a period in the ninth century AD when 'Danish' raiders attacked all along the east and south coasts. The main thing to be said about Lewes at this time is that the raids caused Lewes to happen, but nothing happened to Lewes. There was a raid in AD 892 up the eastern Rother, on Castle Toll near Newenden in Kent. There it was successful, but Lewes was not involved. Two years later the Danish army, returning home, made an attack near Chichester, and the citizens *'put them to flight, killed many hundreds of them, and captured some of them, and captured some of their ships'.*[1] So success in defending Sussex against the Danes had already begun, and if Chichester was in such a state of readiness in AD 894, it is likely that Lewes was capable of looking after itself from then on. *'In the reign of Ethelred II a terrible wave of Viking attacks disrupted the country...'* but *'By 1066 the towns of Sussex are well established and full of life ... they were genuine urban Centres'.*[2]

While the earliest burh ended at the bank and ditch behind Keere and Westgate Streets, by the time of the Norman Conquest the town, *'full of life'*, had expanded westwards as far as St Anne's church. Similar expansion may also have begun eastwards down School Hill to the river.

Much knowledge of the original Anglo-Saxon burh is lost, partly through the natural growth of the town and partly because parts of it must now underlie the later Norman castle. The castle is a complete reversal of the Anglo-Saxon idea of defence. A castle to the Normans was a strong place where a person could defend himself. A Saxon burh was a strong place to which the surrounding country people could run for shelter and defence. So the story of the first town walls of Lewes is that they did their job, and then, when the threat of war was over, they 'went away'. For a long time town maps and the ordnance survey based their depiction of the town's earliest wall on Dunvan's description of the end of the eighteenth century, modified by Thomas Horsfield in 1824. David Freke's excavation of a place where the walls were supposed to run showed that there was no evidence for them. Freke wrote:

> *Three areas 12 x 6m, 12 x 15m and 12 x 6m were excavated. One revealed that the line of the medieval town wall had been wrongly marked and described on maps and in publications from the 18th century to the modern ordnance survey.*[3]

Evidence may still exist, as yet unexcavated, but we must make do with facts from the surviving copies of the tenth-century Burghal Hidage. On this basis Lewes walls had a circuit of 5,362 feet, a handful over one mile. Such calculations have been found accurate for many Anglo-Saxon burhs elsewhere where the wall and ditch can still be traced. At Burpham, the Anglo-Saxon forerunner of Arundel, the line of the walls can be seen and measured, and the formula outlined in the Burgal Hidage fits.

Dunvan's proposed line was mainly near the water-level to the north, east and south. It measures around 6,900 feet long, and so is 1,500 feet more than called for. It follows a river terrace, the three-metre 'lift' above the flood plain, which can be seen outside the built-up area at Landport and Malling in particular. Parts of the line need not be disputed, and are assumed to be Anglo-Saxon.[4] At Burpham the equivalent ditch and bank were about six metres deep and seven metres high respectively, and this gives a spread of some nineteen metres from inside the bank to outside the ditch. The western bank and ditch along Westgate and Keere Streets cannot be a natural feature. These western defences run along the back of

Keere and Westgate Streets, and at their northern end curve eastward along the bank of Castle Lane. From there it is reasonable to project a continuing line past the Elephant and Castle public house to St John's church, because the lie of the land offers no plausible alternative. The strip between Abinger Place and St John's Terrace was still waste of the manor, land in common use, until 1797.[5]

The stretch from the foot of Keere Street to St John's church accounts for 2,700 feet, about half the total circuit. However you arrange the balance, it can only circle the top of the ridge, and would not go down to water-level. The line respects the well-understood tactic that if you want to weaken your attacker, defend the high ground and make him attack uphill. A circuit of around 5,300 feet is a defensible circuit on the higher ground. One of 6,900 feet, down at brookland water-level, would have been many times more difficult to defend.

The manor courts (the surviving records start from about 1594) carefully distinguish between the borough and the Castle walls. The Castle wall is mentioned in 1594[6] and the borough wall in 1603.[7] These dates are close and it seems that two separate structures are described. The Castle wall is well-defined to this day and on the north side is in common with the town defences, while the borough wall is the line at the back of Keere and Westgate Streets. At St John's church, continuing clockwise, all is lost except for conflicting hypotheses. Horsfield's start point for the rest of the circuit is the *'south-eastern extremity of St Johns Churchyard'*[8], and Dunvan's the *'lower end'*. The contemporary map bound in Horsfield's volume, on which all later depictions of town wall circuits are based, shows the wall circling the west and north sides of St John's church without returning back down to the lower or south eastern end. The *'deep ditches and morasses'* of Dunvan's narrative which are supposed to have encircled the whole east side,[9] are described in 1607 as *'... a parcel of vacant land ... three feet wide ... granted* [from the waste] *in 1574'*.[10] The same land is also described as being *'once the town ditch below the Green Wall'*, and describes a drainage ditch at the foot of the river terrace.[11] This can hardly indicate 'deep ditches and morasses'.

Figure 2.1 shows my own, conjectural line for the town wall circuit on its eastern side, taking into account the Burghal Hidage criteria. All I can claim for it is that it is as good as any other, and perhaps better than some. It will require independent corroboration, and could hopefully be more productive than any line looked at so far. Accepting Dunvan's southeastern departure point (if nothing else he is the earliest to try to define the line) for the eastern side of the town, my new line passes through point A, curving above an area once waste of the borough, where the so-called 'Fosse' now runs. Sadly, the claim that the 'Fosse' is part of a Roman camp is unsupported by any evidence. Even now a footpath runs through the southern side of St John's churchyard and has been the subject of countless disputes. It turns down towards the town by the Little Theatre in Lancaster Street, and building development between 1788 and 1799 respected this pathway. Even now it is skirted by the Little Theatre car park. From there the line passes through open ground that was not developed until the beginning of the nineteenth century. There is *'a strong possibility that in the 12th Century the fortified area round St John sub Castro was outside the town ... [I] suggest that the northern boundary of medieval Lewes may lie south of Lancaster Street'*.[12] In a further report Freke concluded that the whole area at the northern end of North Street must have been outside the town, and that any occupation had ceased here by the end of the fourteenth century and was not resumed until the nineteenth.[13]

On the way, at point B on Figure 2.1, the common boundary of All Saints and St John's parishes changes direction in its northeastward line. This change was marked until 1874 with a parish

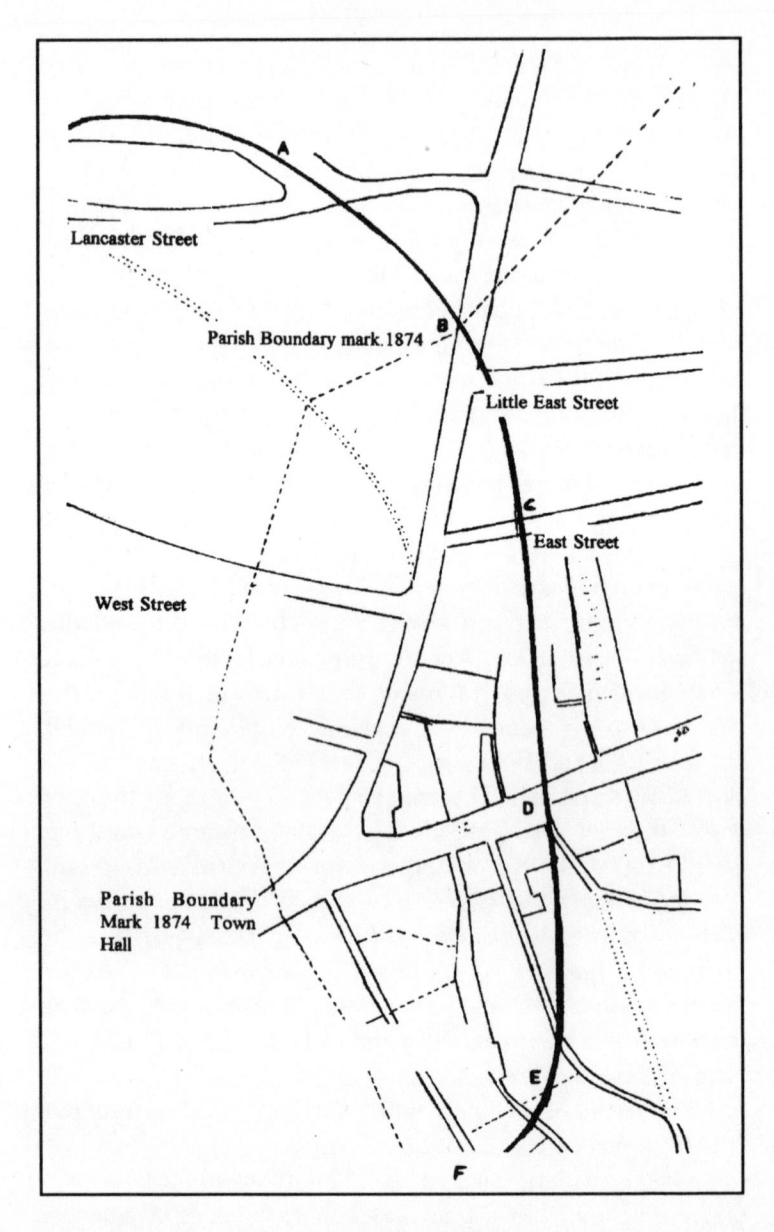

Figure 2.1. *Conjectural line of Anglo-Saxon town wall.*

THE THREAT DICTATES THE SHAPE

boundary marker (no longer in place) just on the far side of the entrance to the North Street car park, by Springman House. At point C the line enters the lands of the High Street property block covering Nos. 201-4, three out of four of which were certainly held by copyhold of the borough, and the fourth appears to have been converted from copyhold to freehold by 1624. Copyhold, a relatively short-term land holding of the borough, is rare and therefore requires explanation for its existence. On the eastern side of that block, visible from the West Street car park, there is a steep drop now forming the western boundary of the houses of Albion Street, which was once held of the manor of Houndean. The copyholding of Nos. 201-4 is a good indicator that the lords of the manor were for some reason reluctant to part with the land on any permanent basis, and chose to retain the power to recover the land for their own purposes. The fact that they chose, in the sixteenth century, to let No. 203 become freehold reflects a dwindling need to retain the land as copyhold. The then owner, Henry Panton, was a medical doctor of some standing in the county, and this may also have influenced their decision.

Point D is positioned on the opposite side of School Hill, between Lewes House and Nos. 28-31 High Street, where Broomans Lane joins the High Street from the south. Numbers 28-31 occupy land not held of the borough, which had come into the possession of the Vestry of All Saints church by 1561,[14] although the body which gave possession is not known.[15] The inference of such vague land ownership, but with church overtones, is that it was a survivor of the time before the dissolution of the monasteries. Certainly Lewes Priory, and the church of Holy Sepulchre (see Chapter Five) owned property in this area, but I have not been able to pin it down to a precise location. At this corner, where Broomans Lane meets the High Street, the ground is still rising. School Hill at just this point used to rise to a steep crest until it was levelled off earlier this century by the Highway Authority. I can recall my real concern as to whether a fully laden bus would make the grade!

Where this rise levels off, the earlier line of Church Lane (now demoted to Church Twitten) used to run through the gardens of Lewes House, and the junction with Broomans Lane lay within the gardens. The actual point is marked by a kink in the line of the boundary wall of Lewes House. The present Church Lane, which meets School Hill between Lewes and School Hill Houses, is a diversion made by the occupiers in 1704.

Between the earlier lines of these passageways was a two acre, triangular croft, reaching down to the boundary of All Saints church, which was held of the manor of Hurstpierpoint. The land was called 'Bugates'. It is now in the grounds of Lewes House, and appears in 1498 as 'Burgeis', in 1582 as 'Bewgates', in 1658 as 'Bugates', in 1685 as 'Boyszgates', in 1697 as 'Boygates' and in 1747 as 'Broomgate'. What is happening here is that a very old name, perhaps 'Burh-gate', has lost its original meaning as the expanding town edged over this area on its way down School Hill towards the river crossing. There are Bargates at Ipswich and Southampton, and perhaps in other medieval towns. At Southampton, the Bargate is still a principal gate bridging the town walls. Although we generally associate the East Gate with the crossroads at the foot of School Hill, there are only two pieces of evidence for it being there. In 1498 there is a reference to '... *in length from the Eastgate of Lewes by the Friars there* ...'[16] This must be what Rowe was thinking about when he wrote in 1624 '... *The Greenewall: between the south end whereof and the ffryers wall opposite on the other side of the street aunciently stood the Eastgate of the Towne*'.[17] Rowe implied that there was no East Gate there when he wrote, so his comment can only be hearsay.

The next indicator, point E, continuing south-westwards

THE THREAT DICTATES THE SHAPE

along the edge of the higher ground through Lewes House gardens, marks a passageway between Walwers Lane and St Nicholas Lane at the southern end of Baxters works, once the site of Nos. 2-4 Walwers Lane. The line then continues past No. 11a St Nicholas' Lane, and links directly to point F where, between St Nicholas' Lane and Station Street, it picks up the southern boundary of St Mary's parish (now the boundary of St John sub Castro and the southern boundary of Caburn Court). Here in Station Street, outside Nos. 11 and 12, going westwards along the line of the parish boundary, I saw in a contractor's trench in 1987, a ten-metre length of almost pure chalk, above and below which was the brownish rubble of made-up ground. This suggests the removed line of the earliest wall or defensive bank. The centre of the chalk was 10.7 metres up the street from the south-western corner of No. 35 Lansdown Place. From there on westwards, the line of the wall behind St Andrew's Place and the County Planning Office follows the edge of a steep drop in levels, and links up with the less conjectural part of the circuit which continues to the foot of Keere Street. Even so, there were grants from the borough waste here as late as the eighteenth century which support the suggestion that the wall circuit then still ran part way up the hill, rather than just along Southover Road.

Moving inside the walls, the defences follow the internal plan of many other Anglo-Saxon burhs. Strangely, their layout is quite standard, although it could be varied to fit the particular topography of the site. *'... the hypothesis that all (these) features in each burh were the consequence of a single episode of urban foundation appears to explain best all the observed regularities'.*[18] In Lewes the ridgeway line of St Anne's Hill, High Street and School Hill ran down to the river-crossing at the high tide level of those days. The presence of the ridgeway was the reason for the choice of site in the first place. The saddle or col of the Downland finger was the weakest point defensively, just where the West Gate was later built, and where the earlier cutting-off bank and ditch were situated. If my view about the East Gate is reasonable, then the town developed from the West Gate along the level ground, to an East Gate situated just where the hill began to drop steeply down to the river.

There would have been lanes laid out at right angles on either side of the central, spinal road, and a lane that ran round just inside the wall. Quite a lot of evidence for this remains in modern-day Lewes. We call the right angle lanes 'twittens'. This is a word apparently limited to Sussex, of which the first part seems to equate with the German 'zwei', for two. I have only come across the word once in any historical document, in the phrase: *'There was lately* [in the fifteenth century] *litigation between William Hore and John Combe over a parcel of land called a twychene, two feet wide, between their tenements'.*[19] The twittens were laid out to give access to the rear of plots of land and back land, where it existed, between the plots and the town wall. They made or became boundaries for the lands lying between them. On the southern side of the High Street the pattern is quite clear, and some lanes do mark blocks of property. The width of these plots is thought to have been twenty feet.[20] Thus between the town wall and St Swithun's Lane, from there to Watergate Lane, and from there to the parish boundary of St Michael's and St John's, each block is 300 feet wide, which allows it to contain fifteen burgage plots of twenty feet each. In practice only fourteen plots seem to have been taken up, ten of the remaining twenty feet being taken up by a central street, and five feet to each of the flanking streets. These lanes at 300 foot intervals do not bear the names of any 'parish' church (there never was, for example, a parish church of St Swithun). Near the middle of each block run central or 'spinal' roads, which are or were later named after churches. St Andrew's, St Martin's, St Mary's and St Nicholas' Lanes are examples. There was probably an equivalent for St Michael's Lane which has also vanished, and

THE THREAT DICTATES THE SHAPE

'Paine's Twitten' may represent its line. If these streets continued north of the High Street originally, the only surviving evidence is a northward continuation of St Swithun's Lane. Most Saxon urban layouts did so. In Lewes much of the earliest arrangement was obliterated by the construction of the Castle. Whatever St Swithun's Lane was called, it certainly continued northwards but became diverted by the second, south-western motte of the Castle, and now runs around the motte ditch. The original line resumes to the north, exiting on Castle Rise, through the line of the combined Castle and town walls. The direct line must have been laid down before the Norman castle was superimposed on it, and was still a public highway until the middle of the last century.[21]

Further east, the parish boundaries of St John sub Castro are known from nineteenth-century maps, as they plunge down into the centre of the town. The width here allows for nine burgages, one of which is occupied by St Mary's Lane and Fisher Street. Further eastwards still, St Nicholas' Lane was probably a spinal road inside the parish, the eastern boundary of which disappeared when St Nicholas' was absorbed into All Saints. One is left with a choice of nine or fifteen plots marking the eastern edge. A fifteen-plot marker would be situated just where Walwers Lane exits School Hill, just inside the conjectural location of the East Gate.

The existence of lanes behind and approximately parallel to the main street frontage plots was an essential part of the urban layout of an Anglo-Saxon town. They are usually referred to as 'common ways', reflecting their use 'in common'. Stewards Inn Lane is an example which forms the southern limit of the plots fronting the High Street between Bull Lane and St Martin's Lane. No equivalent exists on the ground east of St Martin's Lane, but property boundaries suggest continuity as far as Walwers Lane, marked by freehold plot tenures above and other tenures below. There is documentary evidence for such a common lane between St Andrew's Lane and Station Street, known as the 'Gatehouse Way' until at least 1580 when it was enclosed by Lady Ann and Sir Thomas Pelham. Property there was bounded to the south by the 'common street'.[22]

Where there was room, there was also a lane or pathway immediately inside the defensive walls, for which the term 'inter-mural street' or 'wall-street' is now used. This allowed the defenders to move quickly and freely to threatened points of attack, and had to be held in such a way that the free movement of the defenders was not obstructed. While there is still some potential for the idea, there is no real surviving evidence for such an inter-mural street in Lewes, except in the name Walwers Lane. This I suggest is derived from the Saxon 'Weallweg' (wall road) or 'weall-weardian' (wall watching, or guardians, road). Anywhere else, land could be allocated for houses or other defined uses. Oblong plots of land, the 'burgages' (Anglo-Saxon 'haws') were laid out between the boundary lanes, so that the short or 'gable' ends of the buildings faced the High Street. As I have mentioned previously, the rent for each burgage in Domesday was called 'gable' (gablum). In early Lewes charters such lands are described as being held *'of the chief Lord of the fee, therefore yearly all the services due and accustomed'*.[23]

Gable revenues can tell us a great deal. Most manors which held property paid 'gable' at Domesday at six pence quit-rent, but the rent for an area which corresponded to the market place was one shilling. Rodmell parish had forty-four burgages in Lewes at six pence each, while Allington had four but at a shilling each. The borough totals are remarkably consistent, allowing for the fact that medieval mathematics seldom add up correctly! The total rents of assize in Lewes, once fixed, seem to have changed only when the amount of land in occupation fluctuated. Thus:

1086	£9-8-7d 1/2d
1467-8	£9-9-6
1498	£8-1-6
1513-14	£6-8-6d 3/4d
1568-70	£10-6-4
1624	£11-0-6
1682	£11-0-2
1825	£9-0-6 Freehold plus £6-4-2 Copyhold = £15-4-8

(The 1825 amount reflects substantial grants of copyhold from the waste in the eighteenth century.)

The mathematical regularity of this layout is more perceived than real. The High Street is not straight, so the twenty foot frontages needed 'tweaking' to fit. This was achieved by laying out plots so that at a change of direction, if a plot had to have a width of twenty feet at one end, the other would be narrower or wider. This resulted in modifications in the quit-rent, which was reduced or increased accordingly. Two properties were held by 'serjeanty' rents, a token payment for a service rendered beyond the normal. Number 56 High Street, lying almost opposite the old Town Hall stairs, paid half a pound of cummin, and the Bull Inn paid a race of ginger. It is tempting to see these properties rendering some service for the old Town Hall and Sessions House, and the Westgate, respectively. If so (and this is a big if) then the old Town Hall may be contemporary with the West Gate.

So a burgage in Lewes had a frontage of twenty feet and was some 100 feet in length.[24] The 100 foot dimension can be seen today in the property boundaries between the High Street and Stewards Inn Lane. In Southampton it was found that *'smaller tenements, more typical perhaps of the general run of properties in the town, usually averaged somewhat less than one hundred feet in length, with a street frontage rarely exceeding twenty feet'*.[25] The medieval quit-rents for these plots in Lewes were generally sixpence inside the walls, but one shilling in the market place, and this explains the differences between the Rodmell and Allington quit-rents. Outside the walls, in St Anne's Parish, the pattern varies. The mathematics of the arrangement do not look as old as Domesday. Even as late as the end of the eighteenth century conveyances discharging purchasers from other outgoings contained the safeguard clause *'The rents and services henceforth to grow due to the chief Lord or Lords of whom the said premises are holden for or in respect of his or their Fee or Seigniory only excepted'.* As it was, the steward of the manor in 1624 lamented that while the quit-rent system survived in theory, *'... some of these rents are ancient, some denied, none new, thus uncertain and difficult to collect ...* [26]

This is not exclusive to Lewes:

> *'In all the older boroughs there were tenements which paid no landgable, even at the date of the earliest records ... until the rise in values and prices made the retention of landgable a matter of significance and not of worth. Whatever the case in the beginning, eventually the greater number of the tenements paid no burgage rent whatever and many original burgages simply faded away. Freedom from the landgable however made no difference ... to the tenure by which the messuage was held. He was still a burgess and his tenement was held in free burgage.*[27]

Some of these may be missing because of a strict Norman rule that a feudal manor should not extend beyond the boundary of its rape. It would not be the first time that a rule could be got around.

A parallel can be seen at nearby Battle (a post-Conquest, planted town). *'All are burgenses. The basic money rent in the vill is 7d; where this rent has been distorted it would appear to be for other than the favouring of a minority. Thus near the market place the rents are slightly higher than average and certainly more varied, whereas the outlying mansurae tend to pay slightly lower than the average.*[28]

THE THREAT DICTATES THE SHAPE

The original market place is ill-defined in Lewes, but it can be postulated by plotting the values of the quit-rents. In particular the middle of the town would have been a convenient area for a market, where there would have been one or more churches. The usual location is a triangular or Y-shaped area, opening out progressively. Lewes was not a large market town, and over the years there has been quite substantial forward encroachment by the flanking properties into the open space. This was a gradual process spread over almost the whole history of the town. On the southern side of the High Street for example, in 1558 Gatehouse Way ran 138 feet south of the High Street, suggesting that the burgages had encroached forward by thirty-eight feet. Number 53 High Street, (which property I myself occupied for fourteen years), has an entirely new building dating from the sixteenth century interposed between a much earlier building and the modern High Street. The earlier building had for many years been open to the elements at its northern gable end, to judge from the amount of decay in the timbers, suggesting that the original frontage ran fifty feet to the south of the present frontage.

The earliest map of the town (Figure 2.2, hereafter referred to as Randoll's Map) is that drawn by John Randoll in about 1620.[29] Although the original is now barely legible, a good, if slightly edited copy was produced by the town's Amenity Society in 1924, drawn by Walter Godfrey. I have used much information from this map. Once one is used to the conventions employed it can be a very valuable piece of historical evidence. Godfrey described Randoll as having been *'Agent to the Marquis of Abergavenny'*, and says that the map was made for the then possessor of a 1/8th share of the barony.[30] It shows that by 1620, the whole block between Station Street and St Nicholas' Lane has encroached forward towards the Town Hall, accounting for the marked narrowing of the High Street at this point. Evidence of the process on the north side is not so clear, but No. 186 (Ransoms) and Nos.

UNKNOWN LEWES

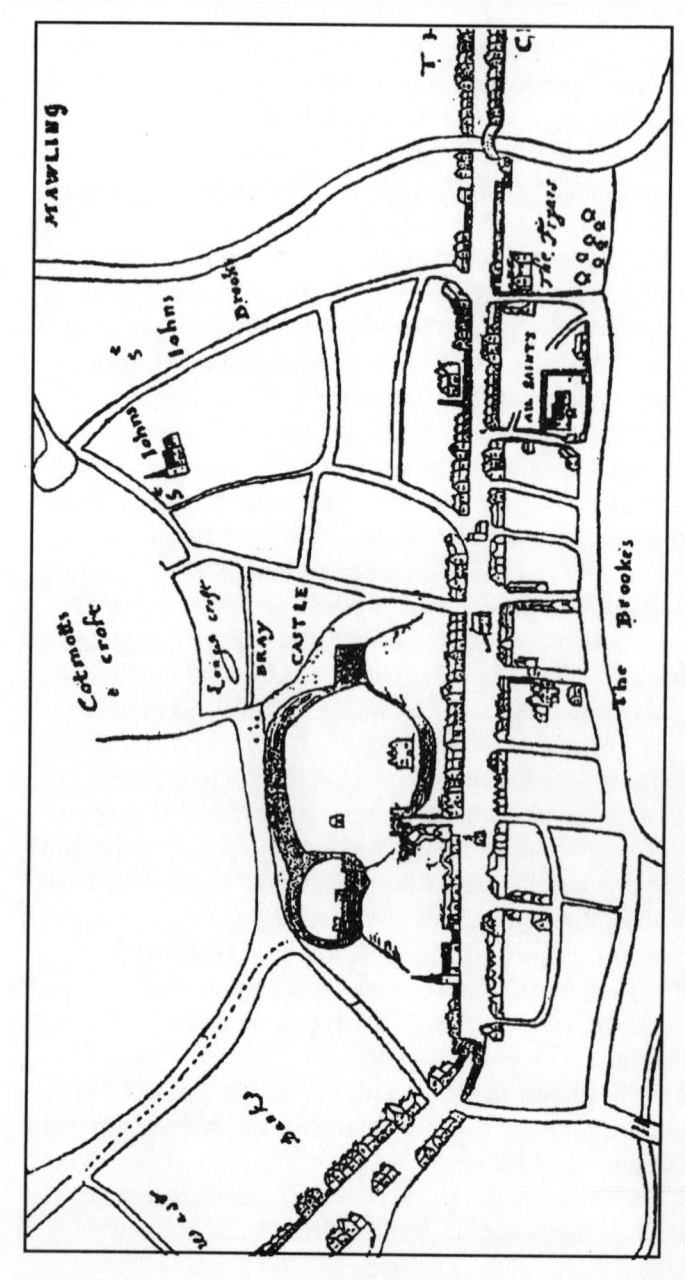

Figure 22. Detail from John Randoll's map of Lewes, 1620.

THE THREAT DICTATES THE SHAPE

187-8 (Lewes Information Centre) are islands of especially highly-rated borough copyhold land, surrounded by land held by outside manors. These two properties represent a forward encroachment of some seventy feet.

It is possible that there may have been more town gates. The layout of the roads suggest that there were. There is certainly documentary and physical evidence for a west gate. In later documents it is usually called the Town Gate, suggesting that it was the only one. There is barely any evidence for an east gate, whether in the area known as the Eastgate or anywhere else. Fisher Street appears once in a document as 'Fishersgate Street', a possible candidate for a gate leading out to the north, much diverted and obliterated by the later, Norman Brack Mount.[31] The earliest gate mentioned in documents is Watergate (In 1256 a property in Southover was described as being outside the Watergate[32]). Therefore Watergate at least may have existed before the assumed construction of the later town walls after the Battle of Lewes (1264). However, the name may have led to a misunderstanding, since in medieval town documents Watergate can be a euphemism for the exit of a town drain. Watergate would have been one of several obvious points for the discharge of waste from the higher levels of the town down to the Winterbourne Stream. Only a short distance upstream the dyke of Southover East Mill (now Garden Street) offered a dry-shod crossing point. The penned-up water behind the dyke would have been a convenient point for taking up water to the town. A postern-type gate seems to have existed in the Castle wall (see Chapter Four) and a gate probably led out towards Landport, from the way roads seem to converge there, at the end of West Street.

Medieval Lewes did not have every nook and cranny filled with houses. Perhaps as much as eighty percent of the area within the walls was open ground. However it was held, (and much was held by outside manors), it could be used for milking herds, layerage for animals for market, storage of timber or other goods, and as the area into which the inhabitants of the surrounding countryside could flee in troubled times.

Waste land in Lewes is thus an important tool, helping us to understand the interior layout. Open land, although described officially as waste, was in use as gardens, orchards, crofts and fields. Waste was not useless land, but land which was not to be used for development. However,

> *In every borough there were areas, bits of no-mans land, odd corners and above all the streets, held directly by no person and called the 'waste'. In the middle ages these were the property of the Borough Lords. Unless he had granted the waste ... no-one might lawfully appropriate it without his permission.*[33]

The bank that was too steep, the verge at the side of a path or lane, was 'waste' in the meaning that we now use. There was also waste which was used in common by tenants of the manor, or by holders of property in the town. Of this little can now be clearly identified because much of it was enclosed early on, but it continues to be described in the borough rentals as 'land once waste', and while it could be granted to private users by copyhold tenure, it could be taken back into the manor if circumstances required it.

Early grants from the waste are distinguished in the rentals as having a fixed 'fine', later ones by a variable fine, and the most recent by a fine and heriot. So from the description of the fine, one gets a rough idea of when the land it applied to ceased to be waste. New grants could be quite detailed, such as one from 1498, let to John Coke for three pence, *'for the herbage and pasture growing and yearly to grow in a disused lane in the parish of St John Baptist under the Castle which was anciently called Laddereslane'.*[34] Understandably the *'Steward and the Lord's other Ministers'* could get it wrong. Land near the Green Wall, let for five shillings and fourpence, had to be released *'because now in common ... and the whole town commonly occupies it, whereby nothing can be levied'*.[35]

Gardens and orchards abounded, most properties having the former at least. Most gardens were small, and were formed by those parts of the burgage that had not been built on. They were storage or stockyards, or productive patches where vegetables, herbs and fruit could be grown. In 1672 Henry Purser leased part of his house on the eastern side of All Saints church to his son, reserving for himself the parlour and the parlour chamber, and *'room in the cellar to lay his beer in, and room in the backside and garden to lay his wood and gather pot herbs for his own proper use'*.[36]

Crofts were the largest open areas. They were really small farmsteads, with barns and other outbuildings. The main croft or field area was the land north of School Hill up to the end of what is now North Street. There were also crofts between East Street and School Hill (now largely built on) and south of School Hill, from the 'Eastgate' cross-roads as far as St Mary's Lane. Many of these crofts may have belonged to the girdle of manors lying outside the town, but this is now difficult to determine. Manorial rights were allowed to lapse, or sold for a cash sum, or sometimes sold with improbably long leases, so later freehold titles leave no record of the original manor. Appendix C lists many crofts, and the manors from which they were held. What the remnants of evidence for the various forms of land tenure show is that the town was shaped largely by outside manors, and this pattern remained substantially unchanged to the end of the manorial period.

Other historians have used the evidence of street names to help determine the early development of the town. This can be a very productive line of study, but pitfalls abound. There is no value in re-stating the pioneer work of L. S. Davey in his *Street Names of Lewes*, which in any case covers a much wider area than this study. There are some names which he omitted, and some corrections which can be made where appropriate. In 1435-6 John Hanmer and his wife were granted 'Middle Lane' in St John sub Castro.[37] Around 1565 John Ottringham enclosed Middle Lane 'from the waste', and the matter thus became a struggle between the manor courts and later owners until 1611, when the record falls silent. It ran between Fisher Street and Castle Ditch Lane, was fifty feet long, and varied between sixteen and twenty feet wide.[38] It remained open space until about 1874, and is now occupied by No. 3a Fisher Street, precisely where a back lane would have crossed. 'Eldestolde Street', around which a minor Lewes names industry seems to have grown up, is a misreading of 'Olde Schole Street', an alternative name for St Martin's Lane, which is also known later as Snellings Lane and Market Street.[39]

For Eastport Street in Southover, Davey's explanation of 'port' with reference to tidal waters is a misunderstanding.[40] Some lands outside the borough boundary had freedom from market toll and other exactions, as though they were within the town. The first evidence of the name is in 1301-2 as 'La Estporte'.[41] The name first appears as a street in the Estporta of Southover near the mill called Watergate in 1315-16.[42] It was in the Southover area that Ralph Broomeman (Broneman) witnessed a deed around 1272-1307[43] and it was here that Brooman Street (Davey p. 16-17) should first be placed. Bronmannestreet (a variation) seems to have moved to its current location in 1353-4, and last appears in Southover in 1316.[44] These sources pre-date the sources given by Davey. His derivation of Brooman from *Planta Genista* may be correct, but it is as probable that Broomeman (Bronman) can claim equal credit.

Watergate Lane is not dealt with by Davey. I have already suggested above a different interpretation from that which is generally accepted. The alternative name for Westgate Street, 'Cutlers Bars', may be explained by the family named Coteler (and variations) extant in Lewes c. 1378-1421.[45] Warner Street (not in Davey) was in St Nicholas' parish. Either it is a lost street name, or may be a variant of Walwers Lane.[46] Warner de Lewes witnesses many Priory deeds around 1200.[47] In 1610 North Street was *'the road leading from the broken church ... to waste between the Brooks and the Lyncke'*. 'Kirkestreete' could be almost anywhere, but seems to have been an early name for a street in All Saints.

'Rormanestreete' (as translated), is equally reticent, but it is described as being on the southern side of the Prior(y) of Lewes, and may appear again around 1532 as *'Brookemanstreet on the south of the lands of the Prior of Lewes'*.[48] This may be a corrupt reading of Broomans Street, and could suggest that Nos. 28-31 High Street (later the All Saints Poor House), was property held of the Priory of St Pancras. There is more work still to be done in interpreting the early pattern of the interior of the town from the evidence of early street names.

Chapter Three
Defence

Lewes the fortified burh seems to have been peaceful up until the Norman Conquest. There is no record of the town being attacked before then.

There are those who see Lewes Castle as the logical continuation of the Saxon concept of defence, but this is not so. The Castle represents a complete change in defence philosophy because it was built by an invader, someone unsure of the success of the Conquest, and someone who sought to defend himself from the local inhabitants. It could hardly have been regarded as a welcome addition to the town. An invading Norman baron, given the military task of holding the Channel coast, would not have been able to cuddle down in the heart of a hostile town. When William de Warenne the elder was assigned the Rape of Lewes, he surely would have needed to construct a temporary castle outside the town.

According to Godfrey, the masonry of Lewes Castle could not have been built until the early 1100s, as a newly-built chalk motte would not be able to sustain the weight of a masonry keep. The only possible reference to an alternative location for a first castle is the Domesday entry for (West) Firle in Pevensey Rape where *'the Castle Wardens have 3 hides and 20 acres'*. One would expect these to have been the wardens of Pevensey Castle, and they may well have been, but Firle is a long way from Pevensey. Also mentioned were two and a half hides held by the 'Clergy of St Pancras'.

No other Norman castle in Kent or Sussex was first built inside an existing town, although some moved in later. If Lewes Castle was first built inside the old burh as most writers seem to assume, then there must have been a special reason for this.

DEFENCE

For the invading Normans, command over the waterways was vital. This had been their route in, and was the way they might need to go back home. With ships close at hand and good communications with the flank commanders, a close grip could be held on the native population.

The Priory Mount, an enigmatic mound of earth south of the railway station, has been suggested as a candidate for the earliest castle motte.[1] Southover would have been a logical site for this. The Dripping Pan, the large rectangular area east of the Mount, is said to have been a salt pan, made from the spoil while digging the Mount, and the Mount has also been claimed as a windmill base. Both of these ideas are unconvincing. It is suggested that the mill pumped up water for the salt pan. The so called saltpan is even now a good twenty feet above sea level, probably more in the eleventh century. There could be no wind advantage gained from building the Mount to site a windmill because the site was and still is open to wind from all quarters.

There is a deed of William de Warenne II dating from c.1090 granting the Priory of St Pancras *'whatever land Bristelm held in the precinct of my Castle'.*[2] And yet the Priory never claimed later to own land in the precinct of the present castle of Lewes, although it was almost ferocious about holding onto any land it had been given. In 1240 a building described as the 'old' hall and chamber within the bailey was repaired.[3] This shows that the main Castle living quarters were in the less rigorously defended bailey, an arrangement that suggests a, by now, more relaxed approach to defence. It also suggests the presence of a 'new' hall somewhere. Some economy in construction was achieved by tucking the northern side of the Castle up against the edge of the burh, on the steep scarp looking north towards the Paddock. This arrangement is not unusual for intruded castles, and it suggests careful insertion so as to minimise effort and cost, and damage to the town itself.

The construction of Brack Mount, the north-eastern motte of the two which make up the castle, may have shouldered aside the earliest line of Fisher Street, a northern exit from the town leading to Landport or Malling. Brack Mount dominates the way into the town from the north, the main direction of threat until the Conquest had established William I as conqueror. This is an important consideration in the pure strategy of castle building. If the threat changes, so the defences must adapt. The south-western motte adds to the strategy only to give better command down the river valley towards the sea, and this implies recognition of a potential new threat from that direction. At its earliest such a threat did not arise until the death of William the Conqueror.

Fitting the Castle into the town without doing too much damage necessitated the careful disposal of the spoil from the ditch surrounding the bailey. The spoil from around the south-western motte seems to have been piled on to the old Anglo-Saxon defensive bank, causing the steep rise up Pipe Passage, fronting Westgate Street. This cannot be a natural feature. It exaggerates the impression of natural strength to the western defence line at the back of Westgate Street. Much of it seems also to have been tipped over the north-facing edge down towards New Road.

It was the succession of William II to his father's throne that radically altered castle strategy. The policy of William I, particularly in the vulnerable but strategically important south east, was to protect and secure his settlement in what was still a hostile land. The apportionment of Kent, Sussex and the Isle of Wight among his closest friends and half-brothers, was a part of this policy. When he died he bequeathed England to William Rufus, and Normandy to Duke Robert. The holders of the south-eastern coastline were faced with a conflict of interest, as the heirs soon began to fall out. Magnates with land on both sides of the Channel could not swear allegiance to both lords, and had to choose between them. Of those barons settled in the great liberties dominating the passage from Normandy to England, only the lord of Bramber Rape was consistently loyal to William II and Henry I. The others, to a greater or lesser extent, opposed the succession planned by William I. Bishop Odo of Bayeux, with the Earls of Eu, Montgomery and Mortain, staged a rebellion against King William II (Rufus) in 1088. William de Warenne I, still loyal to William II, received fatal wounds at the resultant siege of Pevensey castle. It must have been during or after this time, with the threat of invasion from France, that the building of the south-western motte and keep at Lewes was deemed necessary.

William de Warenne II came over from France on his father's death to take possession of his lands and titles. He was to prove less loyal to the crown than his father by supporting the cause of Duke Robert of Normandy against Henry I after the death of William Rufus. In 1096, Henry I had anticipated an attack from Normandy in support of Duke Robert, and the thrust was expected at Hastings or Pevensey. He situated his camp at Wartling, north of Pevensey, but in the event, the attack fell on Portsmouth, and Henry I was able to buy his brother off. Nevertheless, when it was all over, the dissidents stood exposed. The de Warennes forfeited Lewes Rape to the king, although it was later re-granted. They family were now kept under much closer supervision, and de Warenne II had to work hard to convince the king of his loyalty. His support during the decisive battle of Tenchebrai in 1106 helped in this. William de Warenne III vacillated even more than his father. Initially loyal to Stephen during the Civil Wars of 1138-53, he transferred to Matilda, then back to Stephen and finally back to Matilda, before running away on a Crusade, where he was captured and eventually died. Thus he extinguished the direct line of inheritance from his grandfather.

So the lords of the rape were in conflict with the crown at

two periods, in around 1100 and 1140. The most active period seems to have been between 1100 and 1104. Some have suggested that a separate, defensible area within the present churchyard of St John sub Castro was created at this time, when the threat was at its greatest and when Lewes Castle had fallen into the king's hands.[4]

In 1264 the Battle of Lewes took place. It was a battle looking for somewhere to happen, and is not really a part of the history of the town. This ground has been gone over by others and does not need repeating here.[5] The battle resulted in many changes, but for Lewes the principal event was John de Warenne's enforced flight from the town and his inheritances. It is said that before the battle some leading royalists stayed at the Castle with him, while the king made his headquarters at the Priory in Southover.[6] However, a recent study avoids the repetition of a major flaw of past accounts.[7] David Carpenter proposes a route for Simon de Montfort's army from Fletching, through Chailey and Warningore Woods, and then up the scarp face of the Downs to the east of Blackcap to Boxholte Wood, which acted as a forming-up location.[8] This far west, the first available way up on to the Downs would have been from Plumpton, as the routes at Allington and Offham date to a later period.[9]

De Montfort needed to show his men, struggling through the Wealden forests, the best and safest way up. He could have done this by carving a large white cross, the symbol of his army, on the scarp face just below where the path reaches the crest. This point would be visible from a long way inland and in full view as the army emerged from the woods. The cross is still there at Plumpton, now overgrown with grass. The Beamish account of its origins is singularly weak.[10]

This route would have taken the army up onto the top, to arrive on the western side of Boxholte Wood, the best side for a forming-up area in advance of the attack. This theory seems more satisfactory than the usual explanation, that the carved chalk cross is a later memorial to the dead of the battle, erected by the monks of Lewes. There seems no good reason why a memorial, if so raised, should have been placed at such a long distance from the battle itself, facing northwards and away from Lewes. It seems an unlikely activity for the monks to have carried out in any case.

The year 1347 saw the end of the de Warennes as sole lords of the Castle. Almost their last act must have been the erection of the magnificent Barbican gateway, although it is difficult to understand the motive for this since the Castle could hardly be said to be under sufficient threat to justify such an extravagance. A date of 1333-4 has been suggested for the Barbican.[11] It was probably built just after the second murage tax, and perhaps the revenues from that were diverted to it. It would not have been the first time that taxation has been improperly spent. The official guide to the Barbican (my copy is the fourteenth edition) says *'The grooves for two portcullises can be seen. There were also drawbridges to the south, and between the Barbican and the old gate on the north'*. I do not believe there were two portcullises, as examination of the remaining grooves shows that one pair stops at roadway level, while the other continues downwards. This appears more likely to represent a counter-weight groove channel and a portcullis gate channel. The portcullis gate, with the generally accepted spikes at the bottom end, would have been prevented from penetrating the road surface by the groove stops. The counterweight would have been arranged so that it would drop below the road surface when the portcullis was raised, so as not to obstruct the way in. Equally, the 'drawbridge' appears more likely to have been a counter-balance bridge, hinged at the base of the southern arch. Normally level, the counterweight could be freed to swing down, when the 'drawbridge' could then swing up and, in addition to leaving the gulf of the ditch, would close the archway entrance. It would be a delight to see this arrangement fully explained, and if possible restored.

The only known significant threat to Lewes in the fourteenth century was a raid in 1377 by the French, up the river *'to within sight of Lewes'*. The Prior of St Pancras, John de Charlieu, headed the resistance in person and got himself captured. He was redeemed only after a heavy ransom was paid.[12] It seems that the Castle was left undefended at this time.[13] Four years later it was de-militarised.[14] By 1397 it had become the property of the Earls of Arundel, and a description of it from around this time is a perfunctory and unmethodical inventory of arms and materials kept there.[15] In passing, mention is made of a bucket and rope for the well, and various bits of old lead from the roofs of buildings, found in the chapel. So at least we know of the existence of a well, and a chapel, although visible evidence of neither seems to have survived. Fifteen years later the citizens of Lewes broke in and did much damage, and it is particularly disappointing that the Castle muniments were destroyed.[16] Finally, in 1439, the partition of the barony occurred, the Castle then being *'Worth nothing beyond the cost of upkeep'.*

Partition of the Castle was made in 1440 on the death of Beatrice, the wife of the Earl of Arundel and Surrey. It was divided into three parts, the first from the east side to Edmund Lenthall (with free entry and exit), the second part to the Duke of Norfolk, from Edmund Lenthall's part westwards, and the third to Elizabeth wife of Lord Abergavenny.[17] In later years the transitions of ownership of the three areas can be traced back to the three lords.

The Civil Wars of the reigns of Charles I and II were the last major occasions when the castle had a military function. The civil wars had at first sight little impact on Lewes, and equally Lewes had a small part to play in those troubled times. Some information remains in stray sources, enabling us to piece together the story of events in the town during that period. Had circumstances been different and the tide of war swept its way, Lewes would have been ready and able to play its part. The roots of the Civil Wars went deep. They were partly a conflict between Church and state. There was no recorded clash between the town and the Church prior to the dissolution of the Priory and Grey Friars, but the apparent indifference of the town to the fate of these establishments suggests that their relationship had never been close. The earliest available volume of the Town Books begins only a few years after their respective dissolutions. One would have expected some mention of these important events, or at least traces of the consequences, but this is not the case. The Priory precinct and Friary passed to the crown, and thence into lay hands, and there was much other land in the town formerly under religious control which now came under new patronage and ownership.

The town's attitude to Protestantism must have polarised by the time of Queen Mary, in whose reign many Protestants (although none of them from Lewes) were burnt at the stake close to the site of the later Town Hall. Anti-clericalism had been a major motive in the destruction of the Church during Henry VIII's reign. When, under the patronage of Charles I, bishop's clergy and other churchmen raised their heads again in social and political life, the *'jealous laity took alarm'*.[18] It must have been a very peaceful community that listed the town's possessions in 1567 as *'... one auncient* [i.e. ensign] *one drum and one partisan'* [a long-handled double edged spear].[19] These were only ceremonial arms, but from 1587 we see a build-up of arms and ordnance from government sources in order to meet the threat of the Armada. The best list dates from 1591 and includes a gynn (portable crane) to hoist great ordnance, six pieces of cast-iron ordnance, six carriages for them, with cart saddles, horse harnesses and cart-horse bridles. The constables received twenty-one barrels of gunpowder with all the material to ignite it, but one barrel was passed over, on the instructions of Lord Buckhurst (the Lord

Lieutenant of the time), to one Thomas Nicholls *'and other sailors escorting victuals sent over to Dieppe in France'*. Another had been used *'with the consent of the Fellowship'* in shooting the *'great pieces'* in the Castle on the day of rejoicing which followed the overthrow of the Spanish Armada in 1588. There were sixteen small sows of lead, and 120 cast iron shot, of which four had been *'shot away'* trying out the ordnance in the Castle. All of these had gone again by 1596, on the instructions of the Lord Lieutenant, to be shared out between Newhaven and Brighton, being the *'most dangerous places hereabout'*.[20] By 1617 the halberds were *'old'* and by 1637 one of them had been lost.

So, on the eve of Civil War, the borough possessed nothing more warlike than five old halberds, an ensign and two drums. In that year a slow build-up of weaponry began, by this time showing a little more purpose. Six barrels of gunpowder and five sows of lead were bought. By 1641 match (fuses) for gunpowder had been purchased and the leaden sows were being cast into bullets. There was hardly any real sense of urgency, however, for in that year another halberd was lost. Serious provisioning began in 1642. Four *'great ordnance'* with their carriages, wheels and horse harnesses appear. The powder and match, with musket and pistol bullets cast from the lead, had been increased by seventeen bills and halberds, thirty-four muskets and fowling pieces, many *'old and new arms'*, five pikes and *'certain old rests and bandoliers'*. Finally, thirty-two soldiers coats were obtained. In 1642, these all vanish from the town books, yet the return of some can be traced later. By 1699, all the muskets, by then increased in number to sixty-eight, were back in the possession of the constables.

Declining quantities of powder-and-match can be seen, but some was still in the possession of the constables as late as 1703. All these items had seemingly been charged out elsewhere or to individual inhabitants, or stored in a blockhouse or arsenal. A blockhouse is first mentioned in the town records in 1650.[21] The town books also record in 1688 a key for a magazine and two keys for the blockhouse, at the end of James II's reign.

Before 1642, Parliament had commissioned Captain Ambrose Trayton to raise a force of 200 men for the defence of Lewes. The Trayton family were minor gentry living in what is now No. 213 High Street, near the foot of School Hill. Despite later Georgianisation, this is still essentially the contemporary Trayton house of the Tudor period, and in the gable over the west bay behind the parapet there are (or were) the racks and hanging devices for muskets, pikes and uniform coats.[22] This is probably the armoury into which the arms for the defence of the town were transferred from the Sessions House in 1642. In the grounds at the back is also a very small, strongly-built store in use as a strong room. This could well have been either the blockhouse or the magazine. Its small, ogee-shaped window could well suggest a building of this period.

Although Trayton was in direct charge of the defence of Lewes, the main activists during the Civil War and the Commonwealth were Colonels Stapley and Morley. Trayton himself took a very low profile, and his involvement seems to have terminated before the Restoration. After Sir Edward Ford's Royalist success at Chichester in 1642, his subsequent march towards Lewes was intercepted and he was defeated at the battle of Cuckfield. To what extent Trayton and his men were involved is not known. With occasional alarms after 1642 the role of Lewes as anything other than a secure Parliamentarian stronghold seems to have ceased. It provided a secure base for the Parliamentary army, should it seek one, and the Parliamentary Committee did meet at Lewes, in 1645.[23] Herbert Hay from Glynde, William Michelbourne from Horsted Keynes and Anthony Fowle from Rotherfield all represented Pevensey Rape, while William Freeman from

Cowfold represented Bramber Rape. William Newton, representing Lewes Rape, was a prominent Southover resident.

In 1680, Colonel Anthony Stapley wrote *'To the Constables of the Town of Lewes and to every of them. These are to will and require you to deliver the Arms now remaining in your custody in the Sessions House unto Richard Goring of Lewes ... to be by him cleaned and fitted up, and afterwards to be re-delivered unto you etc ... Anthony Stapley'*.[24] Richard Goring was a gunsmith who lived at what is now Nos. 25-6 High Street, and with this little document the story of Lewes in the Civil War comes to an end.

The Castle continued its slow decline. Grants were made from the waste inside it, the earliest being from the 'wall walk' between the Barbican Gate and the south-western keep, in 1600.[25] Thereafter land inside the Castle was steadily converted from waste to individual copyhold ownerships. The present bowling green seems to have been created around 1660, although it was not regularised until 1753, when the Lewes Bowling-Green Society was created.[26] In 1825, Thomas Read Kemp held much of the interior of the Castle. John Hoper, a Lewes solicitor, later conceived the idea of buying up those parts of the Castle which had passed out of the hands of the lords. In a letter of 6 May 1840, he seeks to obtain the last piece of the jigsaw. Hoper gave this explanation in the first paragraph. *'... two years ago I purchased from Mr Kemp the ruins of the Castle of Lewes and the buildings and ground ... and tho' to an indifferent purchaser I would not have resold the property for twice that sum, yet with a view to ensure, as far as possible, the preservation of the most picturesque ornament of our town, I relinquished my purchase to the Lords De la Warr and Abergavenny, two of the Lords of the Borough, and to Lady Amherst, at the price I had paid'*.[27] In fact this had been his plan all along, acting for the lords at arms' length.[28] At that time the keep was occupied by Kemp as a dwelling or summer house. The *'southern tower'* contained an entrance hall, dining room, chamber and a servant's chamber. The *'western tower'* had two rooms described as Mrs Beckett's rooms, Mrs Beckett being known from elsewhere as an aged retainer *'who shows the Castle'* and who was to have security of tenure.[29] Although rescued in this way, uses for the Castle were limited. Mr John Farrant's article in the Sussex Archaeological Collection No. 134 provides an authoritative view of this matter.

In 1849 when the Sussex Archaeological Society first sought to obtain a tenancy, the Castle was by then let by the lords to the Hon. Henry Fitzroy (an MP for Lewes) who was apparently using it as a gigantic billboard for his election advertising, causing much adverse comment. By 1850 the Society had obtained a lease, and the subsequent history is more that of the Society than of the town. The Society took down and rebuilt the barbican parapet, unblocked the machicolations, restored the stone copings, and opened up three arrow slits which had been blocked. Much additional work was done to the keep, and there can be no doubt that the Society is responsible for the fine state of repair in which this remarkable building is now kept.

As an aside, in 1824 the South Saxon Lodge of the Freemasons were granted a lease for fifty years (at the modest rent of five pounds per annum) to use the rooms in the barbican as a lodge for free and accepted masons. They seem never to have occupied the hall built on the site of the northern bastion of the West Gate up to then, but let it to various persons. With about half their lease still to run, they were reported on adversely by a committee of the Society for defaulting on the obligation to repair stipulated in their lease, and after some pressure had been exerted they left the Barbican Gate by 1857 and held their meetings first at the White Hart and then at the Crown Inn.[30] The present Freemasons Hall has a plaque on it with the building date of 1817, but this refers to an earlier building and not the one visible today which was built in 1868.

Chapter Four
The Management of the Town

By Domesday, Sussex had been separated into administrative divisions called rapes. It had been a separate Anglo-Saxon kingdom only up to the eighth century AD, and when we now talk about 'Sussex', and sing 'Sussex by the Sea', it is not always clear what we are referring to. These former kingdoms are not, and never have been 'shires'. The rapes took their names from the principal settlements, but while the names may be pre-Conquest, the exact areas covered by the Domesday rapes seem to date to the post-Conquest period. Rapes were divisions of Saxon origin, since the Domesday Book refers to Lewes Rape in the past tense.[1]

The administrative counties of East and West Sussex are a creation of 1888 and we can learn little from them of the earlier system. In Lewes, the administration of the town grew directly out of the administration of the rape. Lewes Rape when we first encounter it in the records was administered by its sheriff, the king's deputy, and this office continued in existence until the fourteenth century. Lewes and Shoreham had been the customary centres from which the sheriff administered the whole area, and it was not until 1274 that the jurors complained that Richard of Cornwall *'attracted'* the county court to Chichester, *'to the grievous loss of the whole Shire'*. The sheriff's royal power gradually weakened, and his function became more closely identified with the barony, as the rape and the town gradually passed into the hands of the de Warennes. Often, the same people held the various offices, but the management of rape and town were separate. It was over the rape that the barony exercised its control, and over the town that the manor of the borough did the same. Richard de

THE MANAGEMENT OF THE TOWN

Playz, a major landowner in Lewes Rape, owed attendance at the county court each month, and at the Earl of Warenne's court at Lewes every three weeks. Officers of the household and barony of de Warenne are known from about 1190, but they served their part also in the management of the town. In 1240 a steward, Sir Waryn de Kingestone and a porter, Robert, were mentioned.[2] These two officers were among the most senior of the Norman barony. The steward was the chief officer of the earl's household, while the porter was the military commandant of the castle. The Latin term for porter is *janitore,* but the title derives from the keeper of the door (*portus*) of the Castle. By 1256-7 the de Warennes had their own private sheriff, Hugh de Plomton, who was presumably not a king's officer.[3] In later years the steward of the barony was the steward of the castle and of the manor, and Thomas Lancastre held all three titles in 1471.[4] The steward's functions were outlined in about 1265 when Roger de Loges handed over to his successor, Richard de la Vache.[5] He wielded great power. Acting as the earl's personal servant, he chaired the barony court, required the bailiff to take action, and directed persons to ascertain facts. He instructed his successor to respect any agreement made in his own time. He condoned or excused individuals, distrained for offences if he saw fit (or possibly if he was bribed enough), but he could also order possessions to be sold.[6] It seems that not all officers were paragons of virtue, or held in high esteem. *'Even as the children of the night - the owl, the nighthawk and the vulture - love darkness rather than light, so from the King's Court are set Sheriffs, under-sheriffs and beadles ... men who at the outset of their office swear before the highest judge to serve honestly and faithfully God and their master, but being perverted by bribes, tear the fleeces from the lambs and leave the wolves unharmed.'*[7]

In 1278 the steward was Oliver Fitz-ernis. The sheriff's bailiff had arrested him for some unknown offence and confined him to Lewes Castle. From there, with the connivance of Hamelin, the porter, he contrived to escape. Interestingly, the source refers to the escape via a postern gate, and this is the only evidence of the existence for such a gate.[8] The escape was hardly surprising, since the porter and the steward were 'brother' officers. Hamelin was an adventurer, paying for his appointment and making what he could out of it. Here is evidence for the earl's most important officers conniving directly against the king's sheriff.

The steward carried out his functions from Stewards Inn. Close to the Castle, the inn with its offices, living accommodation and stables fronted the High Street between St Swithun's and St Martin's Lanes. The area between Bull Lane (now called 'Paine's Twitten') and St Martin's Lane, south of Stewards Inn Lane, contained the steward's croft and pigeon house.[9] These areas were assigned for the use of the steward of the barony from the time of his earliest appearance. After the third failure of the male line of the de Warennes in 1347, resulting in the partition of the barony among three lords, the steward's office lapsed, to be replaced by a separate steward for each of the three lords. They then operated from their lord's principal manors, looking after all of his lands. The croft, the inn and stables lost their single purpose, and were let out. By 1462, John Southwell held the croft, described as lying west of a plot called the Old School House, which lay in the angle between Stewards Inn Lane and St Martin's Lane.[10]

Stewards Inn is said to have been destroyed by a fire in 1593, but this is pure folklore.[11] The evidence for the fire is a record that states that, five years later, Daniel Johnson gave up to Richard Savage *'a garden once built upon and lately consumed by fire'*. However, the dimensions given follow exactly the small, oddly-shaped garden at the back of Nos. 76 and 77 High Street.[12] This garden paid a fourpence rent, and was additional to the rest of the hospice and stable block, and seems not to be related to Stewards Inn. On the other hand,

Nos. 74-77 High Street all seem to contain parts of the original structure of the inn, and Nos. 74-5 apparently formed most of the fourteenth-century building, now much altered. The date above the dragon post in St Martin's Lane is, unusually for such dates in Lewes, probably correct.

The last time the croft was let was in 1589-90, and it disappears out of the manorial record from then. Yet in 1623, William Clagett Sr. (then living at Nos. 82-3 High Street) provided a settlement gift of *'... an orchard or piece of land with a pigeon house, called Stewards Inn'* for his son's marriage with Mary Newton of Southover. This was three roods (i.e. 3/4 acre, 32,670 square feet) which takes us about two-thirds of the way down St Swithun's terrace. Beyond there southwards was borough waste until 1750.[13]

The Alfredian, burghal functions of law and order operating in Lewes, left a legacy which has been carried down to the crown and magistrates' courts today. The Justices of Assize were first instructed by about 1166 to travel 'in eyre' and sit in every shire court once every seven years or so. In Lewes, by the end of the eighteenth century, the town was looking after them with some care, providing two armchairs, and *'... cushions, squabs, green cloth etc. ... including two earthen chamber pots for the Accommodation of the Judges at Assizes'*.[14]

They continued to come, and as late as 1715 the town government was petitioning for the assizes to be held more frequently. This did not reflect a desire for any speedier justice, but was a recognition of the value of the extra business they brought to the town. For the next thirteen years the judges and their clerks were entertained at the town's expense, by subscription raised from the townsfolk. Concern was expressed on several later occasions at the risk of loosing civic functions. The mayor of Lewes protested vehemently in 1889, when the first meeting of the new East Sussex County Council was held in Eastbourne. All subsequent meetings have been held in Lewes![15]

Keepers of the Peace appear from about 1277, and the office became fully regularised by the Justices of the Peace Act in 1361. They met four times each a year, giving rise to the term 'quarter sessions'. A reinforcement of their functions took place in 1461, when all the indictments previously held at the sheriff's 'tourn' were transferred to the quarter sessions. This surrender by the barony of a major part of its' authority meant that control previously exercised by the sheriff passed to the county magnates. By 1531 the justices were dealing with the Poor Law (the foundation of modern county government) and from then 'county' power was in the hands of the magistrates. The 'Knights of the Shire' of the eastern part of Sussex (and the lawyers advising them) not only congregated in Lewes, but had principal town houses there, to serve both their own interests and those of the law.

The office of porter may have disappeared by 1398.[16] By 1371 a new officer, the constable, appears. There were two constables at the head of the town administration from at least the sixteenth century. The first named constable was John Northampton in 1394, when he is clearly described as *'constable of Lewes Castle'*.[17] In 1476-7, Richard Luke, constable of the Castle, was paid an annual fee of £6.13s.4d by the Duke of Norfolk for the term of his life.[18] By 1499 Thomas Gaston is described as *'one of the constables'*, but by 1542 two constables are *'of the burrough of Lewes'* and are clearly the town officials found later at the head of the town government.[19] Some semi-royal officers appear fitfully in the records. In 1397 Thomas Podheye was the *'Kings weighing officer for the weighing of wool'*, foreshadowing the control to be exercised later by the clerk of the wool market.

The third Earl William de Warenne died on a Crusade in 1149. By 1147-8 his brother Rainald had, in his absence, and with the agreement of the Prior of St Pancras and the barons of the earl, restored by charter the merchant gild.[20] Prudently,

Rainald provided that if his re-grant was not valid, the earl (or his son) would have to confirm it. Rainald provided for the existence of a son, but if there was such a son he did not live to inherit. The earl did not return and the earldom passed in succession to his daughter, Isabel. Rainald's grant may have continued to be valid, with the gild later enlarging its functions under another name, that of the 'Fellowship'. The Fellowship would have begun as a court for the regulation of the market and trading generally, a true function of the pre-Conquest merchant gild, the only borough 'court' for which the charter is the document of evidence.[21] There is no doubt that a form of town government did exist in the early sixteenth century, it did carry out a number of functions and it had existed *'time out of mind'*, which has the meaning of beyond living memory, and in a legalistic sense, before 1189. John Rowe was at least in the legalistic sense very precise and it is doubtful if he would have used such a term carelessly. 1189 was the first year of the reign of Richard I, forty years after Rainald de Warenne had restored the merchant gild. There would have been a continuing function for it to perform, so in Lewes *'time out of mind'* must date back, in this case at least, beyond the watershed of AD 1189.

By the time records are available, we see a body of town government called the Fellowship, having very little power, and then only for those things which the lords found to be boring or unprofitable. The Fellowship consisted of twelve of the *'wealthier and discreeter sort of townsmen'*, and may represent the successors of the jury of twelve official witnesses known from the pre-Conquest burhs. The numbers were flexible but they were *'never so fewe as 12. nor more than 24. and upon death or removall ar supplied by the eleccon of the greater number of the subsisting societye'* John Rowe wrote, *'... out of which Society according to his seniority, the younger is chosen by thelder (with the consent of the greater nomber of the Jury) out of such of that society as were neuer formerly constables wthin this Burrough (for never was it knowne that any man was twise yonger constable or twise headborrowe)'.* [22]

They became known as either the Fellowship, or the Society of Twelve. The forcing-ground for the membership of the Twelve was the junior Society of Twenty Four (never to be more than twenty-seven). The members of the Twenty Four had to be invited to join the Fellowship. This was confirmed in 1595, with the proviso that their election should be *'not any more in the Castle for the avoydinge of further disorder'.*

The candidates would spend at least a year in the probationary society, during which time they had to behave respectfully towards the Twelve. Only one list of names of the Twenty-Four seems to have survived from the year 1611, when they confirmed new articles. They also had to do *'all other service that the rest of that companaye have usually done'* which does not help us a lot. Any offences against these rules meant that they would be locked up in the Westgate prison (following a majority decision by the Twelve) for three hours, or fined. The society was organised as a self-appointed oligarchy, benevolent or not. Much was made of the obligations of the members, and the Whit Sunday and Monday social aspect was an important lubricant in the management of the towns affairs. The principal festivities took place on Whit Monday, but preparation started well beforehand. The constables arranged for a Fellowship supper for themselves, and also for the Twenty Four. On Whit Sunday new members were admitted into the Twelve, and after evening prayer the resultant gaps in the Twenty Four were filled. The new members had to listen to the rules set for them, and then qualify by taking part in the Watch and Walking on the following day.

The ceremony of the king's (or queen's) Watch and Walking was an important element in the pageantry of the town, introduced in 1285 under the Statute of Winchester, and the outward and visible manifestation of one of the internal obligations of the borough, the Assize of Arms. Each townsman between fifteen and sixty years of age was required to keep some weapon or effects to help maintain the peace. In 1612 in a roll of *'several armours and furniture'*, William Inyans (described as parson of St Martin's, but correctly parson of St Peter Westout), had to provide himself with *'a musquet furnished'*.[23] It was the duty of the constables to inspect this assize of arms, which in Lewes took place during the Walking ceremony.

Led by the crier and the constables, the headboroughs were followed by the Twelve, who were obliged *'... to wear a gown and other decent and comely apparel fit for ancient townsmen'*. The headboroughs were the right-hand men of the constables, and had to do most of the dirty work. They collected the town tax, they had to carry some offenders to 'The Gate', and set others in the stocks. They carried long staves of office, which are still maintained in the Town Hall council chamber. The stave of office was a necessary item of equipment, a symbol of the authority carried by the bearer. In a time when there were no uniforms, and town government was very much a personal affair, the staves of office were their only recognisable manifestation of power.

Those newly-elected to the Twelve marched with the Fellowship on the Monday. They were followed by the drums of the borough, and the borough officers and clerks of the markets. Then came the Twenty Four, and after them the citizens and inhabitants with their furniture of arms and weapons, which needed to be in serviceable condition for inspection. If members of the Twenty Four wished to establish credibility for their eventual admission to the Twelve, their attendance was compulsory.

When the parade was over, both societies adjourned to their suppers, which they had to pay for themselves, although a rent for the 'broken church' of St Nicholas was also used.

Sometimes, out of love for the town, money would be given towards the cost of the suppers. In his will of 1555, John Cotmot left two shillings for each of four years for their Whitsun night supper, and he also left a property to his neighbour for two years, with two shillings of the rent payable to the constables.[24] The constables had to tell the Twenty Four where and when their supper would be, although it is not clear whether they dined together or separately. Evidence for the exact nature of the ritual is thin, but in 1815 there were changes made, so that the rent of the Town Brooks, Hangman's Acre and other income was to be divided between the constables' dinner, and the subsequent event, called the Affairing dinner. *'Immediately after the removal of the cloth the Headboroughs elect (who at all times are to act as Stewards on these occasions) do see the expence of the dinner from every person who has dined.'* Any guest who was not an inhabitant had in addition to pay for a bottle of wine, and the stewards had to make sure that the free 'liquor' consumption was kept within the amount of money collected, after which all present had to pay for any additional drinks.

Lewes was a seigneurial manor without a charter, holding the usual manor courts under the supervision of the manorial lords. When we first get access to documents, it is clear that the Fellowship ran in parallel with the normal manorial courts. The court baron was firmly in the hands of the earl's stewards, and dealt only with copyholds held of Lewes manor, ignoring transfers of land held by other manors or tenures. Suitors at the Court Baron attended before the bailiff (or bailiffs), and the court was held under the chairmanship of the steward, as and when there was enough business to justify calling it. Around four or five resident copyholders were sworn in as the 'homage'. The bailiff himself or the homagers would introduce the matters to be dealt with before the steward. He heard, decided and disposed, acting for the lord or all the lords. He determined the fine to be charged for the court's approval. We tend now to think of a fine as a punishment, but then it was a payment marking the conclusion of the business. The bailiff's function was to account for the profits of farms (property which was let at a profit rental over and above the manorial quit-rent), the market tolls, the profits of the courts themselves, and chevage. The last was an amount paid for permission for townsmen to live outside the manor, or for outsiders to live within the manor. Ralph Briscoe, the Earl of Dorset's bailiff, accounted in 1618 to his 'receiver', the steward, for his chevage. [25]

Interesting information can be had from copyhold grants of land made from the waste to freeholders. Permission was given in this way to erect railings in front of premises, probably to keep out cattle being driven to market. Thus at the 1618 court Thomas Trayton was granted a strip three and a half feet wide and ninety-six feet long, before houses lately owned by Comport, his brother-in-law. We can identify the existence of the property, and from this can see precisely how much frontage it covered, now represented by Nos. 211 and 212 High Street, and part of No. 210. At the same court Godard Brode was granted land seventy-two feet long and thirty-two feet wide, to the east of his property in Keere Street, between the property and the town wall. This covered the outer bank of the town's western defence, now behind and parts of the gardens of Nos. 6-10 Keere Street. (Grants made from the waste all along the backs of the eastern side properties of Keere Street can be traced from as far back as 1430.)[26]

Of the important buildings, the old Town Hall and Sessions House was the most important, and leads us through history to the Town Hall of today. It was the hub around which all civic functions revolved. Clearly the need would have arisen for a meeting place where the Fellowship, the jury and visiting justices could discharge their duty. On Randoll's Map of c.1640 the earlier Sessions House is shown in the middle of the High Street, just to the west of the Star Corner crossroads. On that basis it was opposite Nos. 50-54, not as is sometimes claimed opposite the White Hart, within St John's parish.

In 1542 the town had a box or chest in which important documents and money were kept.[27] The constables were responsible for the safe keeping of this box, one holding the box and the other the key. In 1565 they paid thirteen shillings and fourpence for *'making a place for the justices of the assizes to sit'*.[28] Godfrey interpreted this as the provision of temporary accommodation while a Sessions House was being built.[29] If so, he is suggesting that the custom of providing a place for the justices, and possibly the existence of an earlier Sessions House, goes back to the years before 1564. Rowe recorded that town charges could be used for repairing the Sessions House, but he also says that this is no novelty and is one of those charges *'about the town'* which may be made and continued *'time beyond all memorye'* for the public good and use of the borough. By 1575 there was in the Sessions House a *'treasury door'*, presumably some cupboard for the safe keeping of the box or its contents. The usher was paid one shilling for opening the door on each of three occasions in the year, hardly an onerous or even profitable occupation. In 1592 the town box is listed in the inventory along with the *'keyes of the cubbordes wherein the evidences of the town doo ly'*.[30] In 1668, when the justices acknowledged that there was no precedent for the inhabitants paying for repairs to the building, they effectively recorded their ownership. In 1696 and again in 1729, they affirmed that the three eastern rapes (Lewes, Pevensey and Hastings) should repair the building. In exchange for being allowed the use of the building for civic purposes, the Lewes Fellowship voluntarily assumed responsibility for some interior repairs and decoration.[31]

Whose building was it, who paid for it, who could use it? Dunvan thought it belonged to the town, and that the magistrates used it for quarter sessions on sufferance, even though *'the bench of eastern Justices ... have threatened to exclude the Borough from holding meetings there'*, an attitude which he regarded as wanton usurpation. In fact, the town government seems to have been careful to have use of the building without taking on any obligation to maintain it. Any contribution made to repairs was always at someone else's cost. Rowe noted in 1564 that the constables paid out ten pounds for timber *'towards building the Sessions House'*, yet none of the £12.5s.0d in the town's balances is recorded as having been spent on materials.

Twenty-four years later the town government paid for *'new lofting over'* of the Town Hall. This must have represented some improvement involving ceiling over the upper room.[32] Little more than 100 years later, the justices in quarter sessions confirmed that expenses paid by Lewes inhabitants in repairing the Sessions House should not be regarded as establishing any precedent.[33]

Figure 4.1 shows the edge of a successor to this building that the town has now sadly lost. Paul Dunvan, with his usual overkill, describes it as *'a perfect nuisance on account of its very improper situation and a monument to the stupidity of those who fixed it there'*.[34] It was by then a stone-quoined brick structure about fifty-four feet long and twenty-four feet wide, rising thirty-three feet to a cornice.[35] The ground floor had an open eastern half, and there was a court room and perhaps other rooms on the upper floor, lit by seven windows set in round-headed arches. These upper rooms were approached by an outside stair at the western end. An illustration dated 1761 exists of a building said to have been erected by John Morris, Lewes, builder and stonemason, of which there were two, father and son. Whether what is seen is a building of 1696, or of 1728 or 1761, is not known. My guess would be 1728, and thus the work of the father. It was in July 1728 that the clerk of the peace for Sussex issued a notice from the quarter sessions that the building was so out of repair

Figure 4.1. "The Church House of John's, Lewes. Corner of St Mary's Lane", as seen from the Town Hall and Sessions House. Lambert, 1778.

that steps should be taken to remedy its condition. The work and the costs of the outside repairs was to fall on the *'Eastern half of the ... County of Sussex'*. It was probably this building of which Dr John Burton said, in 1751 *'... I observed that the public buildings being very old and dirty with nothing venerable or ornamental about them ...'* [36] In 1808, for the reason given by Dunvan, it came to the end of its useful life. It was the magistrates who pulled down and sold the building, and paid for the new one.

This was the County Hall, on the northern side of the High Street, now the Crown Courts. The town was again allowed rights over the new building similar to those it had enjoyed over the old one, but these amounted to no more than the right to make use of the premises, which it seems has now been lost.

Important and more profitable town property functions were held firmly in the hands of the lords of the manor through the Court Baron. There must have been some underlying record of all freeholders which would have been necessary to keep a control over quit-rents payable. In 1619 Robert Drewe was distrained by the bailiff to come to the court baron to do fealty for No. 174 (part of Nos. 174-5) High Street, a property he had bought, although it was freehold.

The other court, the View of Frankpledge, allowed the Fellowship to exercise its true function. Also known as the Court Leet, it was usually presided over by a bailiff, or occasionally a steward. It was here that the Fellowship appeared *en bloc* before the view, calling itself the *'Jury to enquire for the King'*. It was able to act as a jury for a royal court, dealing therefore in matters of statute and record. In these courts one can see how the lords of the borough kept control, particularly over any revenue, but delegated the less rewarding work. In this the Fellowship exercised power in a way that looks like a direct descendant of the old borough moot. While the presence of a merchant gild and town government is a peculiar feature of medieval boroughs, it cannot be taken for granted. *'The essence of the original gilds was an association of owners, freemen-burgesses, merchants and capitalist masters, securing their vested interests...'*[37]

Most ancient boroughs of a similar age to Lewes sought a charter of incorporation, leading to the setting up of the office of the town mayor and the like. Lewes may have tried to obtain a charter, but it didn't get one, because the de Warenne's didn't want it to. To them Lewes was a private manor over which they retained lordship rights. In some towns the merchant gild, or its equivalent, effectively 'bought' the town from the lords.

The Court Leet or View of Frankpledge was referred to sometimes as the 'View', or more normally as the 'Lawday'. It was a strange hybrid since the original function of Frankpledge was the control of the divisions of an Anglo-Saxon vill into tithings, where ten families bound themselves corporately for the behaviour of each member. In most examples it had by now lost that function. In Lewes the court met formally only once each year at Michaelmas, and the real work of the View took place officially on the first Monday after the feast of St Michael (although in practice it was variable).

The officers of the court were little different from those of an ordinary manor. The difference is not that they existed, but how they were appointed. At the Michaelmas meeting, the approval of appointments by the lord's stewards was by tradition a formality, but symbolic of continued feudal control. The View was therefore a rubber stamp for the election of the officers and members of the Fellowship. The senior and junior constables chose their own senior and junior headboroughs *'without any contradiccon or alteracon by the Stewardes'*, so long as the feudal principle was clear.

The View had the right to deal with offences against statute law, where the power had not been passed down to the Fellowship, or drawn up to superior courts, and with some

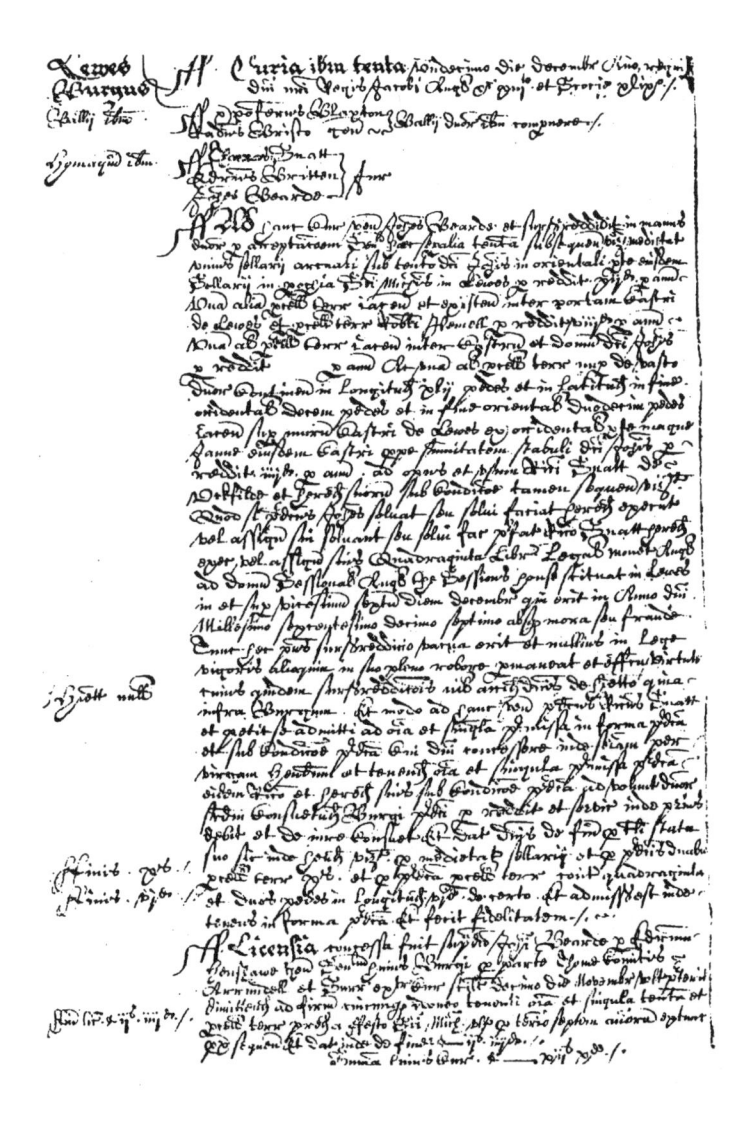

Figure 4.2. Example of proceedings of the Court Baron, 1615-16.

specific town ordinances involving revenue for the lords. It is instructive to watch a typical session of the View, in order to experience the full flavour of what must at times have been a sort of pantomime. The records for the court of 1588 has been chosen as a representative example, and some evidence from other court records have been introduced where they provide useful additional information.

Thus when the Fellowship appeared at the View, they immediately changed themselves into 'the Jury'. The Jury appointed the principal officers, but only after nomination by the Fellowship (i.e. themselves), on the steward's assurance that he would not refuse to accept them. The manor thereby retained its authority, but delegated the work. The View dealt with such matters as the appointment of market officers, which suggests that the Fellowship was in existence before or in the earliest days of the market. As a market existed before Domesday, this is likely to represent a precious survival from the past. In 1588, Christopher Blaxton, the Earl of Abergavenny's bailiff, took the chair, accompanied by Richard Marks, bailiff for Thomas Sackville, Lord Buckhurst.[38] The bailiff for the Earl of Arundel was not present. The constables, with their headboroughs and nearly all the 'Twelve' then appear, almost at the end of their year of office, as the jury. All of the Fellowship were supposed to attend, but there follows a list of five not present. That the five who were not present were not fined was presumably because only twelve were needed for a Jury, and the Fellowship totalled twenty in that year. William Marshall, a headborough, had died during his year and had been replaced by William Reade.

Fortunately it was the custom for the other court, the Court Baron, to list all residents whether present or not, up to 1614, and those lists are available. They were compiled from Lewes Bridge to the boundary at St Peter's at the western end of the town, naming each property owner as the compiler came to it, either on his left or right. This is very useful since it gives an approximate idea of where most people listed lived. Next follows a list of the residents, described as *'the men of the borough'*. Twenty-three were not present *'within this view'*, and were fined two (old) pence each, except for two who were (without explanation) fined threepence, and one who has no sum against his name. On any normal system of arithmetic this should produce four shillings and four pence, but produced a stated total of only three shillings and sixpence, illustrating the difficulties involved in making sense of this sort of document.

The View then got down to business, dealing first with offences against the statutes. The jury presented Brian Nicholson as having committed an assault on a constable, thereby drawing blood *'against the Queens peace'*. Similarly Richard Bishop and John Bachelor had assaulted one Peter Lewis, also drawing blood. There was no discussion or judgement, no defence or pleas in mitigation. Nicholson was fined five shillings and the others one shilling each. Clearly assaulting a constable was the more serious offence. Perhaps the hearing had taken place elsewhere, perhaps before the Fellowship, and in the judgement was accepted at the View, which merely approved the sentence. In other examples the hearing appears to have been held before the magistrates.

Further offences against the peace were also sentenced by the Jury. The first was presented by the pinder or pound keeper, Roger Miles. The same John Batcheler with his servant had broken open the lord's pound, where William Burrell had impounded a horse found on his property called the Barley Banks. The pinder and William Burrell would normally have shared the fee for releasing the horse, but instead Batcheler was fined one shilling. Some of this may have gone as a reward to Roger Miles. At the time, the manor pound was situated at the extreme western end of the borough, in St Peter Westout parish, moving in 1800 to an area in St John sub Castro. Another offence was presented by Daniel Johnson, clerk of the wool market, who claimed that John Ade had killed ewes not fit for human consumption. Ade was fined a shilling, but already the distinctions between the various markets were becoming blurred, since this would formerly have been a function of the clerk of the butchery.

There ended the *'offences against the statute'*, and the court turned its attention to local offences. These were dealt with in groups. For putting *'sullage and filth'* opposite their gates or next to the Castle ditch or gate, thirteen householders were fined twopence each. John Batcheler was again among them! The names are useful because most of them can be identified as people living in houses on the northern side of the High Street.

Five more put sullage and filth at Aylards Corner. They too were fined twopence, but obviously dumping there was becoming a serious matter, since Rowe records that in 1605 a special penalty of ten shillings was introduced for one offence. A John Aylard lived at this corner between 1513 and his death in 1544, but the first official reference to the name of the corner is later in 1588.[39] Two more were fined fourpence each for dumping at Stewards Inn, and one (twopence only) for having a gutter running out of his premises. Next came a group of those who, having been fined at some previous court, had either not paid or had not amended their ways. William Hawkes was presented for, among other things, failing to mend his privy near the queen's highway. It must have been quite expensive for him, since he forfeited ten shillings and was fined a further thirteen shillings and fourpence, and was ordered to have the work done before Christmas.

Ten more residents in different parts of the town were fined for sullage or gutters. Then came Thomas Gynnes, John Austin and William Storer for not having removed timber which they had dumped in the High Street. They lost their previous fines and had the same fine reimposed. Of course, it being close to the onset of winter, one would expect stocks of firewood to build up, and it could be that fines cost less than any rent likely otherwise to be charged.

So some attempts were made to preserve hygiene in the town, which were not limited to the *'scouring of the town dyke'* mentioned by Rowe, probably a communal obligation. There was a 'town dyke' by Westgate Street, a 'sink' or castle ditch in Castle Ditch Lane, a common watercourse or common sewer on the northern side of the town, all of which were the responsibility of individuals or certain groups.[40]

'Common Tipplers' were inhabitants running unlicensed alehouses, and were proceeded against, but it was easier to get a conviction if they were charged with selling drink in unmarked measures. The ale conners of the parishes were responsible for checking measures. On relatively rare occasions, persons were presented to the court for being drunk. These were no one-night indiscretions, but related to drunkenness over quite a long period. Richard Smith forfeited five shillings in 1615 to the poor of the parish of St John sub Castro, having been drunk for one month. He was again before the court in 1619, with a drinking companion Robert Fell, both having been *'commonly drunk in the last six months, and to be punished according to the form of the Statute'*. At a time when nearly everyone brewed their own beer (it can be seen from property descriptions that brewhouses were almost as frequent as wash-houses and privies), it is hardly surprising that the odd surplus barrel was sold. From there it was a short step to selling by measure, legitimately or otherwise. The ale conners would present offenders by charging them with selling beer in measures which had not been sealed, since an unlicensed seller was unable to achieve this. Seventeen people were fined twopence each for being *'common tipplers of beer'* and thereby breaking the assize. In 1598, confirmed in 1651, the inhabitants of the borough obtained at the quarter sessions an act for repressing the 'great number' of alehouses. No new licences were to be issued within the borough or in the parish of St Mary Westout except at the request of the constables and

Fellowship, who would present and certify the licensees as fit persons.[41]

Three others fined were common bakers of bread, the offence they had committed being selling at less than the standard weight for loaves, as set by statute. In 1649 the constables presented to the Easter quarter sessions that *'upon the severall complaints of the inhabitants of Lewis, Millars who take much more toll in these deere times than is their due'*, and listed among them William Willett *'that farmes at Kingston Mill'*. He was fined twenty shillings.[42] Many people were fined for allowing their pigs and hogs to wander around through the streets and lanes of the town. At subsequent courts the same people appear again and again, suggesting that although it was an offence against town ordinances, it was perhaps a good way of getting the streets cleaned up a bit, while raising revenue for the court. Lastly, a resident had encroached onto a road, the location not specified, *'to the nuisance of the queen's people'*.

The Jury then reported that *'otherwise all is well'* and proceeded to announce the new officers for the coming year. The principle was explicit that *'The constables ... make choice ... of all the other officers ... without any contradiction or alteration by the Stewards'*.[43] The fact remains that whether contradicted or not, the steward had the authority to approve the new appointees. In addition to the constables and headboroughs, the pinder, and the clerks of the corn, fish and butchery markets were appointed, and also the searcher and sealer of leather. The scavenger, and four ale conners, one for each parish, were appointed next. The scavenger was responsible for seeing that the streets were kept clean, and a town by-law required that between the Westgate and St Nicholas, every inhabitant must keep the frontage onto the High Street clean, the fine for not doing so being sixpence. The distance between the Westgate and the Broken Church includes the Market Place. The scavengers eastern limit was extended by 1682 '...

to the house of Mr John Holney att the lower end of Schoole Hill' (modern No. 17 High Street, and No. 210 opposite), thus reflecting a continuing eastward drift of growth.[44] Although not appearing in the official borough records, a borough chimney sweeper was buried in St Michael's in 1770.

Yet another duty pressed on the constables was that of dealing with vagabonds. Many displaced wanderers had been roaming the country since the dissolution of the monasteries, augmented by the soldiers and sailors discharged after the Spanish wars. Some care of them was needed to ensure that they did not become a burden on the community.

Overseers of the poor were created by the end of the sixteenth century, and while the collection of the poor rate seems to have been left to the individual parishes, the procedure for moving them on away from the town was in the hands of the constables. To this end they equipped themselves with a device for sealing their documents, called the Vagabond Seal, which first appears in the town possessions in 1576. Vagabonds sent away would carry a sealed document requiring them to return to where they came from, and specifying how many days journey was allowed. In that year the constables *'disbussed ... for ye pooer: as basterd children and impotente peopell ...'* some sums of money.[45]

Quite a lot had taken place beyond the routine business of the View. A boat belonging to one Goram had discharged a cargo of munitions into the hands of the customs officer at Newhaven, one John Brode, who in turn passed them to the constables on the last day of January. Amongst the cargo were forty-two barrels of gunpowder, of which twenty had been handed over to Lord Buckhurst for use by the Lord Admiral in the defence of Newhaven against the Spanish Armada. Only one barrel was for the defence of Brighton, an interesting illustration of the relative importance of the towns at the time.

The river frontage south of Lewes Bridge was the town wharf. From the thirteenth-century murages it is clear that

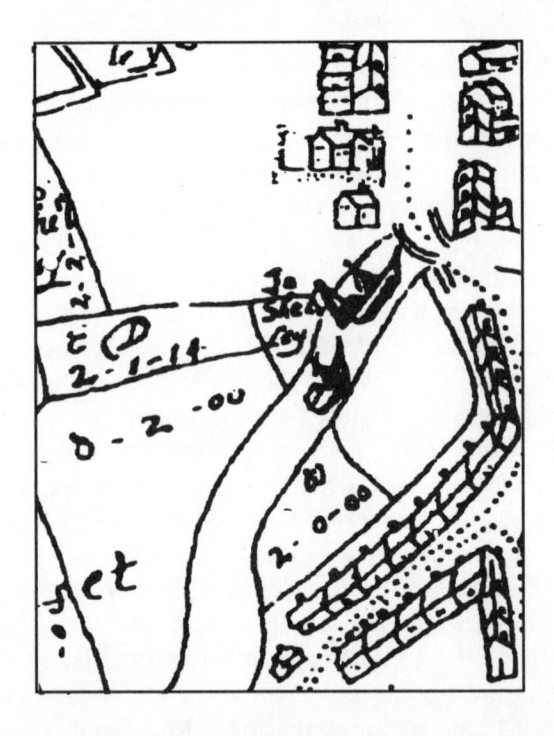

Figure 4.2. A detail from Deward's seventeenth century map showing ships at the town wharf.

barges were coming up to Lewes by this date, and the riverbourne traffic may always have been a feature of the town's economy. The trade reached its height after the construction of the lower Ouse navigation at the end of the eighteenth century. The wharf lay between Railway Lane and the river, and Randoll shows some buildings here with archway entrances. Deward's map of the same period shows ships docked here, one with two masts and therefore of a respectable size. The land here was not already owned by the borough, but there is an entry of 1628, when the constables were authorised to receive forty shillings '*towards money by them disbursed unto the Surveigher of the hauen*'.[46] In 1802 a passing reference in the Town Books records '... *that the Publick Wharf at the Bridge belonging to the Borough be forthwith put into a state of good repair'.*[47]

The appearance of the West Gate is known only from a time when it was already in ruins. However, there is a plan in the Lambert Collection at Barbican House which shows not only the West Gate, but how the centre was removed to allow for traffic (Figure 4.3). It shows two principal bastions, each with three arrow slits, facing respectively inwards, outwards and ahead, giving cover to central entrance. On the outer edges of both bastions were narrow passageways leading to small pedestrian gateways through which access could be gained without the central gates having to be opened. Where the passageways entered the bastions, the presence of jambs suggest a door and a little niche which probably served as an outstation of the market, a collection point for market dues, or at least a check-point. The main and the two subsidiary gates would have been closed at night. None of this arrangement is visible in Horsfield's illustration of the western elevation.

The lords allowed the Fellowship the use of the West Gate, or at least its northern bastion, as a town gaol, particularly for *'suppressing disorderly conduct',* but they had to find part of the cost of upkeep. The lords also authorised their bailiffs to pay on the Affeering Day 6s 8d, for the *'cryer and spittle'.* Presumably the crier was the town crier, who was not a borough officer, and the lords therefore maintained control over him. What the payment for the spittle represents is not clear, but was seemingly some contribution towards the upkeep of the poor house at the Spittle crossroads.

So it was after the Lawday that the Fellowship, acting for the first time in its own name, held the Affeering Day to confirm the new appointments made. On the Affeering Day the Fellowship had a clear function to perform in its own right. Strictly speaking it should have taken place immediately after

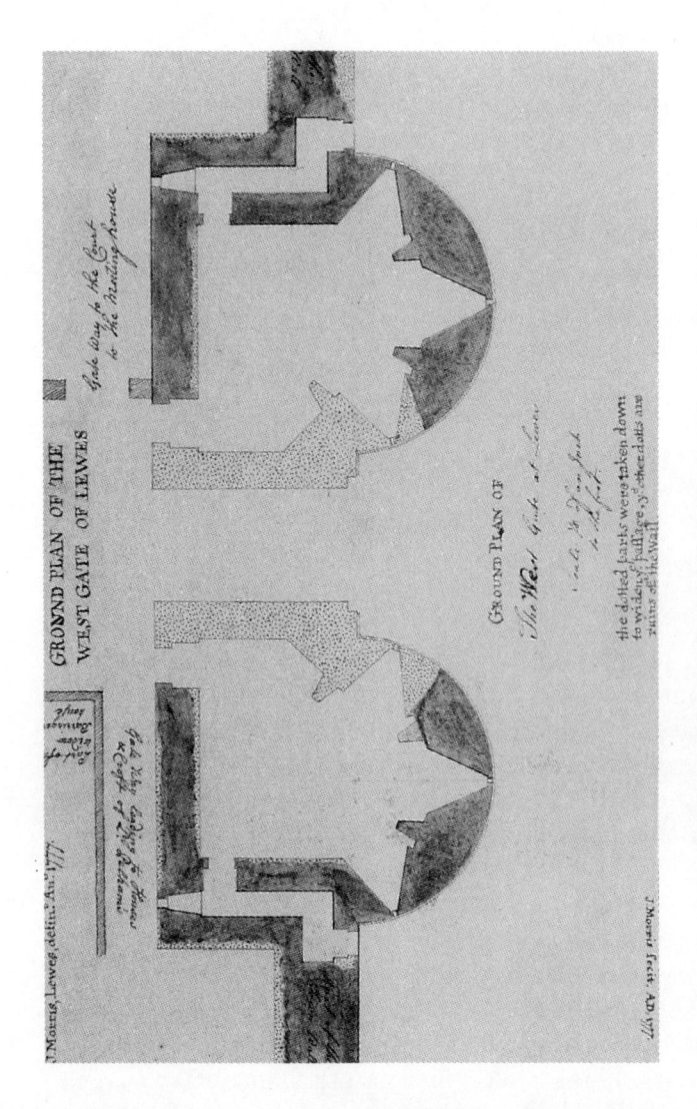

Figure 43. Drawing by J. Morris, 1771, of the remains of Westgate, showing the centre parts removed to widen the passage.

the View, but the proceedings mention various dates on or after 10 October.[48] They checked (or as we shall see, failed to check) the inventory of the town's possessions, and the accounts of the retiring constables and Headboroughs. Any balance of money was passed over to the new constables, and so began a new year in the administration of the town. During the year the constables accounted for the receipt of twenty-two pounds and two shillings. They had *'disborsed and layde out'* for new lofting over the Town Hall, for handling all the munitions and sundry expenses. Twenty-two pounds and two shillings seems a remarkably neat balance, and a balance appears so often that one is left with the impression that they spent the money first, and then drew in a balancing amount by taxation. They recorded the handover to their successors of the town's possessions, and all the munitions received, although then and later the munitions float in and out of town control until they were all struck out of the record. This transfer of the town's possessions was often indolently carried out, with as much inattention being paid by those who received them as those who were accountable. An example of how the efficiency of the process was impaired, if 1632 is anything to go by, is found in the final account of the constables. This *'... was brought in by them and the particulars of it delivered to Mr George Segar to ingrose in [this] book, which is not done by him because he saith he has lost some of the particular papers'*. One would have expected Mr Segar to be more conscientious after that public reproof, but in 1635 *'It was ordered Mr Segar to enter their accounts who did forget it and so was no particular account entered the same time'*.[49] As late as in 1848, when John Hoper the Steward presided, *'afterwards they adjourned to the Record Room where the property of the Borough was transferred and the accounts for the past year submitted'*.[50] Presumably there was yet another supper, since Rowe noted in 1624[51] that the lords of the borough allowed their bailiffs, at the Affeering Day, to contribute (and account for) ten shillings towards the supper.

Where constables spent more than they collected, they had to find the balance out of their own pockets. Internal disputes could be settled by the constables and the Fellowship without reference to the lords or the stewards, who frankly did not want to be bothered with petty matters. Payments were made to the clock keeper, and the bell ringer, who does not appear to be the same as the town crier, may be associated with the nocturnal perambulation.

The town clock appears in different locations around the town over the years, to St Michael's and then the Market Tower, and the bell moves from St Nicholas to the Market Tower. The bell is still there, called 'Old Gabriel'. The market clock was later installed in the bell tower of St Michael's church, after the Market House was given up. Contributions towards the costs of the maintenance of the Sessions House, the ruined church of St Nicholas, the Market House, stocks, pillory and whipping post, were met fully or sometimes only in part. A pillory was set up in 1570, and the Broken Church was let by the constables in 1571 to Robert Stuckell.[52] The town inventory of 1646 lists four keys to the Sessions House gates, which would have been the metal grilles limiting access to the otherwise open ground floor.

The accounts of the Fellowship distinguished between 'necessary charges' and 'particular expenses'. Particular expenses were once-only or unusual items, and these required specific approval. The accounts for 1568 seem to show a degree of openness not otherwise apparent in the procedures of the town government in the sixteenth century. Then the constables were 'allowed' (i.e. this was a particular expense) for *'carting and whyppinge of dyvers lewde persons'* and for *'putting a boy to prentice'*. The town books that still exist date from 1542, although the entries up to 1576 are said to have been copied from older books kept from 1264. This claim, if true, indicates a great loss to us, and it may have been one of the earlier accounts books which is laconically dismissed in 1688 as *'the booke with ye parchment cover ... not delivered to the new constables'.* [53]

In 1573 the constables let their common brook, known as the Constables Brook, setting out a rent and some tenants obligations. In 1584 they let ground called the Town Brook, of about one acre. Both of these were *'beneath St John sub Castro church'*, close to the common spring.

Between Brook Street and the river was an area of brookland, apparently held by the manor of Malling, outside the boundaries of the borough. It was divided into a number of parcels of land. In 1568 six meadows totalling eight acres *'in the meads below St John sub Castro church'*, were bounded to the west by the public droveway (now the footpath past the swimming pool to Willey's Bridge), by the meadow of the town of Lewes to the south, and the common sewer to the north. These eight acres included one acre of brook *'near the common spring'* let in 1573 by the constables and Fellowship, to the citizens of the town. This parcel was called the Town Brook. The terms of the lease made it clear that they had held the land for some time.[54] In 1603 John Rowe records that he had *'granted'* to the constables further brooks containing two acres. However one manipulates the evidence, it is difficult to see how he could have had any freehold title to grant, since the land was held by Malling. He was probably trying to help by creating a title deed where none had previously existed. In 1601 Francis Jefferay of South Malling conveyed to John Rowe, who was then a member of the Fellowship, three pieces of brookland totalling two acres, and the turnaround time of this conveyance, from the grant to Rowe of 1601 to the grant to the constables of 1603, is quite speedy for the time. These two acres became known as the Constables' Brooks, and these and the Town Brook (at least by 1667) were held in trust by named persons, the rent to be paid towards the costs of the constables' feast.[55] In 1860 the constables and headboroughs

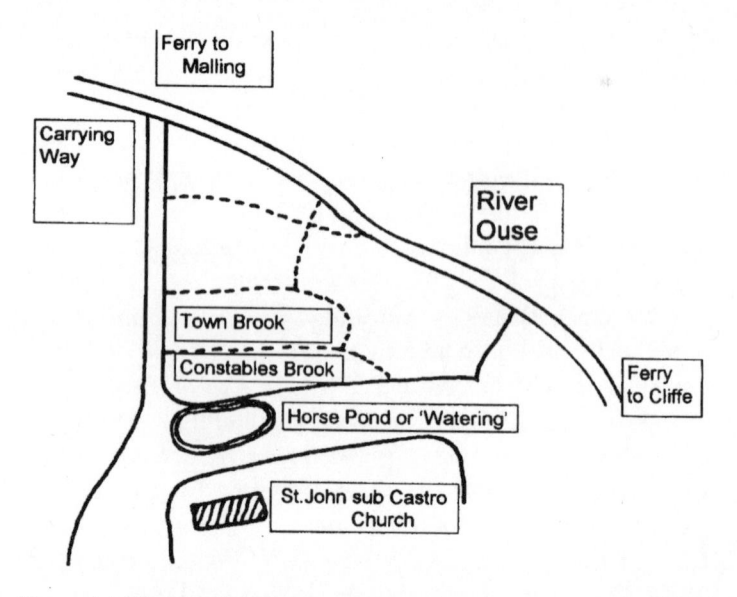

Figure 4.4. The Town Brooks

promoted the building of a public and safe place for bathing.[56] Having no funds for this purpose, they made an appeal to their fellow townsmen and, finding that their appeal had been *'most liberally responded to'*, they were able to go ahead with the proposal. Probably because of the insecure title to the land, they resolved in 1884 to enquire into their ownership, with a view to it being conveyed to the Corporation. At the south western corner of the Town Brooks, just beside the public droveway, was *'the watering'* or the Horse Pond. It seems to have been a principal spot for watering animals. This appears on some maps to be inside the borough boundary, but on others to be outside it.

As civic pride increased, so the town's fire-fighting services grew in importance. Buckets and shovels have already been mentioned, but in addition there were *'ij great eyrne whockes wth chaines uppon them & two greate poles mad ffor the yovse of ffire if nede Reqvyre wthin the tovne'.*[57] The two iron hooks, with chains attached, mounted on poles, were used to pull off burning thatch, or even to bring down burning buildings. It was not until 1680 that the inventory suddenly sprouts *'three ingines one great and two small'.*[58] In 1730 these had shrunk to one engine, and another smaller, both given by Thomas Pelham in or after 1726, with leather pipes. The big hooks had increased to four.[59]

What happened to Thomas Pelham's gift is uncertain, but by 1783 another engine had been obtained by a subscription organised by the constables, with a promise to get yet another.[60] One such fire-engine is now on display at Anne of Cleves House. They were then stored in an 'engine house' provided in 1784 by Thomas Kemp in what is now the Gun Garden of Lewes Castle. But even by 1800 the Fellowship had not appointed trustees to the property thus given,[61] and not unnaturally the benefactors son, Thomas Read Kemp, objected to this inefficiency, and demanded the return of the land. With much protest the Fellowship resolved to give it back in 1818, and to build their own engine house (with room to store the borough's records and other property), using fifty pounds offered by Mr Kemp. The site chosen was on the eastern side of Fisher Street, and had been held of the manor of Southover.

By 1550 there was a dispute over the structure of the town's administration, and at the Whitsun feast new *'articles and orders'* were drawn up. In 1595 the articles were again renewed, but this time in greater detail. These then governed (or quite often failed to govern) procedure for many years. The new articles laid down that the Twenty Four should in future be chosen in the Town House and not in the Castle. Perhaps some disorder led to this change, but by then or shortly after, land inside the Castle was being let to individuals, and it may indicate only the clamping down on use of the Castle as public open space.

In 1595 the constables' new articles required them to perambulate the town at least once each week from October to March to search the inns and alehouses *'and other suspected places where any bad and disordered rule is ... kept ...'*[62] This requirement lasted until 1793, possibly more honoured in the breach than in the observance. In 1793 the *'inhabitants'* (as the Fellowship tended by then to call themselves) decided to arrange a night-watch of the streets, backways and lanes in the borough. They engaged three men at seven shillings per week each, to work between eleven at night and six in the morning. Only two were on duty at any one time, and they were provided with two warm great-coats, two felt hats, two large horn lanterns, and two watchmen's ratchets. Presumably the off-duty member had to freeze. Hand bells were also accounted for, one for the bellman and one for the crier (along with the criers badge and staff of office).

A second and much greater upheaval for the Fellowship came in 1799. William Lee Jr. (bookseller and the publisher of the *Lewes Journal*) was appointed in 1778 to the position of senior headborough. He seems to have performed his duty more conscientiously than most of his predecessors. Increasingly, querulous notes began to creep into the town records, culminating in an outburst on his appointment in September 1799 as senior constable. This involved a pointed attack on the work of his predecessors. He used such phrases as *'unaccountable neglect and political abuse'*, *'utter subversion of original constitution'*, *'shameful degradation'*, and so on, and then began a campaign of investigation into the whole process of town management. The full story runs from page 104 to page 128 of the second volume of the Town Book.[63] It is too lengthy to extract here, but is fun to read.

New constables were eventually appointed, but there can be no doubt that from then to the demise of the whole system in 1881, Lee's whirlwind foray into the proceedings of the Fellowship left an indelible impression. What really provoked him was the discovery, in the shop of a London cheesemonger who had bought a lot of possessions after the death of Serjeant Kemp of Malling, of the Deed of Trust from Steere's charity, dated 1682, which was property of the Fellowship and of which Kemp had been a trustee. Lee had arranged a fresh deed of trust and appointed new trustees, only to find that the earliest deed was still in existence.

This display of incompetence betrayed a degree of mismanagement of many properties given in trust to the town. Steere's charity had been granted out on a long lease, contrary to the terms of that trust. Money lent to Mrs Board and Dr Tabor in 1707 had not been repaid, and the charity had received no interest for many years. Many other examples of mismanagement were exposed. Based on William Lee's investigations, a new town inventory was drawn up and published at the Affeering Day, which now took the shape of a public meeting held at the Sessions House. Lee's meticulous list of details presented only seven days after his original public attack on the system, had presumably been some time in preparation. This included a reference to the 1717 library gift from Rev Joseph Graves, by this time the subject of almost total neglect. The Town Hall, to which the town had no title, was surrendered with the keys, some specific furniture and the use of the lower court. This freed the way for the justices to arrange its demolition and the building of the 'County Hall', now the Crown Courts.

Lee's parting shot on the appointment of new constables was to put on record that some of the town's possessions *'... though of considerable antiquity and highly worthy of presentation, do not appear to have been mentioned in any former account, and for what reason we cannot say'*. The of Lawday was then adjourned to 15 October, when they resolved to clean up the mess, and in one body to perambulate the bounds.

The meeting examined the items of the town property which were missing, dealing with *'the few remains of the town's property which have escaped the hands of fraud and official negligence'*.

In 1806, arising from all this, the many clauses in the Lewes Cleansing and Paving Act set out to eradicate offences against which the jury of the Court Leet had previously shown themselves impotent. Much more than the mere paving of the streets was involved.[64] Among the many clauses were ones allowing the commissioners to put up street names at the ends of each street, and it is from this time that many of the names then in use became 'fossilised'. Among the prohibitions were included one against the making of any bonfire, or letting off, or selling, or giving away, any firework. In view of the national reputation of Lewes as the foremost centre for fireworks, presumably this was as impotent as most other attempts at legislation have been. They were also empowered to number the houses, and from this the first numbered street directory of 1812 must have been compiled. An original list is held in the Sussex Archaeological Society library at Barbican House, but there have been many changes since 1812. This caught out Walter Godfrey who describes some properties with street numbers relating to the one next door.

There can be no doubt that William Lee, with the support of others, set a number of cats among some ancient and complacent pigeons. It was good for the town, and for the local historian, because the information brought out at the time is a valuable source. The Fellowship was left as something of a paper tiger, but it struggled on. Sometimes it was efficient, sometimes it was indolent, sometimes it seems to have been corrupt. The Fellowship that Rowe knew had existed time out of mind, and it was still functioning in 1881 on the eve of the incorporation of the borough.

Chapter Five
Church and Parish

This chapter mainly concerns the parishes of the borough of Lewes. The Westout parishes and Southover will be dealt with in more detail in Chapters Eight and Nine.

In 1337 the Bishop of Chichester (who in Lewes held only the church of All Saints) was trying to strengthen his position, and published a never realised plan aimed at setting up new arrangements covering all of the Lewes churches.[1] He began by pointing out that most churches in the borough were *'diminished impoverished and unserved'*, whilst avoiding mentioning that this was due to neglect by their patron, the Priory of St Pancras. The suggestion has been made that the neglect was due to the depredations of the Black Death. This cannot be true, however, as the Black Death began around a decade later.

The bishop proposed that St Mary in the Market and St Peter the Less should be united with St John sub Castro. By this means, any of their parishioners who held burial rights in St John sub Castro, since *'time immemorial'*, could be confirmed in those rights. 'Time immemorial' in the early fourteenth century really looked back into the distant past, and is a less precise term than *'time beyond the memory of man'*, which refers to an earlier period. The bishop went on to propose that St Andrew's and St Martin's (where both churches had burial rights by custom in the churchyard of St Michael's) should be merged into All Saints on the death of the then incumbent of St Michael's, with St Michael's losing its burial rights.

Then he listed Holy Trinity, St Nicholas and Holy Sepulchre churches and proposed that their parishioners and those of All Saints on the southern side of the High Street should continue to enjoy burial rights *'as hitherto has been accustomed to be done',* but that all revenues, tithes etc. should thenceforth accrue to All Saints. It is strange that, after the use of such clear and explicit language, the last phrase should be so imprecise. It almost implies that the bishop did not know what burial rights were involved. The plan suggests that those parishioners on the northern side of School Hill should be merged into St John sub Castro, retaining the burial rights they had enjoyed there *'since time immemorial'.* Burial rights meant that the parent church was entitled to burial fees from the smaller churches, so that even if they were able to conduct burials within their own building, the parent church would still receive the fees. The parochial limits were given as the house of Robert le Spicer on the west, and Cliffe Bridge on the east. The house of Robert le Spicer was identified by Godfrey as the Star Inn, later the Town Hall, part of which is the westernmost house in St John sub Castro, on the northern side.[2]

Another essential document containing much useful information about the early parish layout is a nineteenth-century map which shows the parish boundaries at that time.[3] Figure 5.1 shows the map, with the boundaries emphasised, although there were several alterations to them before the map was made. Apart from the extra-parochial precinct of the Castle, the town was divided, then as now, into the *'four parishes in one leet'* described in the Court Rolls. These were the core parishes of St Anne, St Michael, St John sub Castro and All Saints. The parish of St John the Baptist, Southover, although not part of the borough, was intimately connected with it. Excluding for the moment Southover and the Westout parishes, the parishes of the borough as seen on that map acted as 'mother' churches for smaller churches at one time within their boundaries. Ecclesiastically, the Castle precinct was separate, and there is no way of knowing how rigorously this was applied, since for borough manor purposes the precinct was divided between St Michael's and St John sub Castro. It is almost as though the Castle precinct was devised to prevent

CHURCH AND PARISH

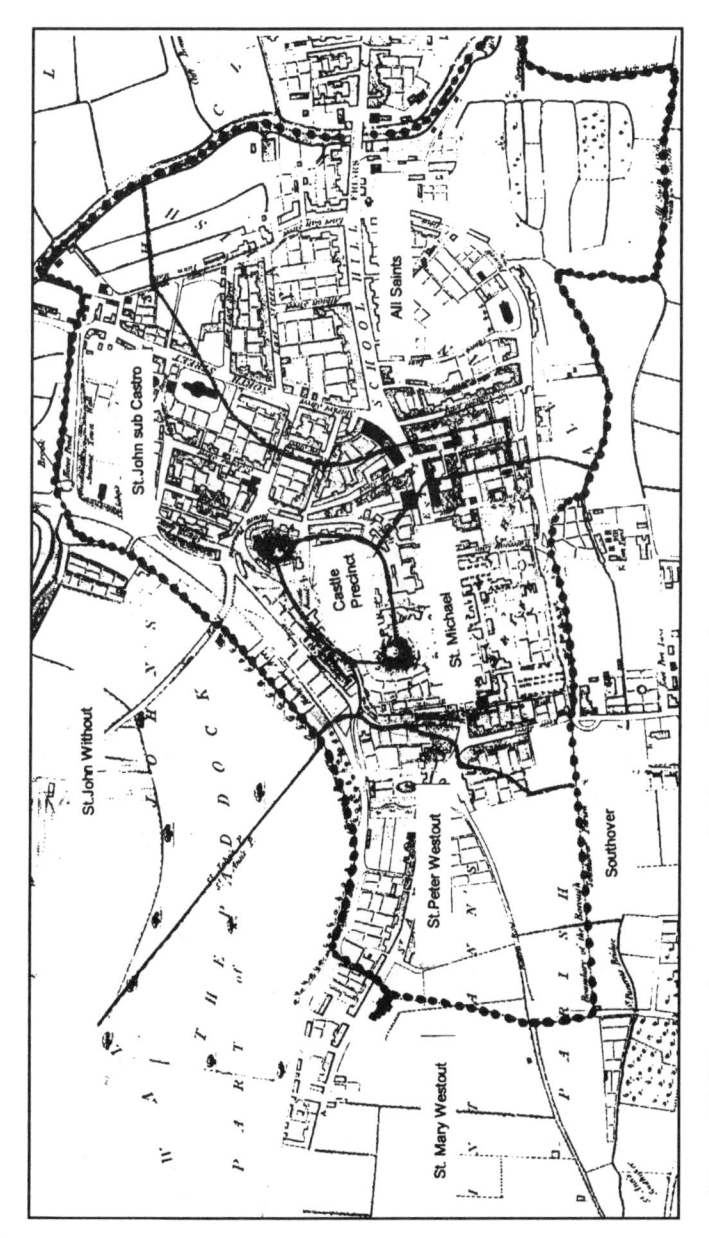

Figure 5.1. Nineteenth-century map showing parish boundaries.

arguments between the parishes about baptism and burials of the residents. In his 1736 will, Benjamin Court, resident in the precinct, makes clear that he is *'of the Castle of Lewes'*, although he is of the parish of St Michael's in lay transactions, and a member of the dissenting Westgate Chapel in matters of worship.[4]

A third useful source is provided by the early charters of the Priory of St Pancras, in which most of the Lewes churches are named.[5] Before his death William de Warenne I gave to his newly founded Priory the patronage of the two Westout churches of St Peter and St Mary, later united as St Anne's. He also gave the tithes of two other groups of churches, which his son later converted into a gift, to mature after the death of the then holders. The terms of the gift were that a western group, consisting of Saints Martin, Andrew, Mary, Peter (the Less) and John sub Castro should pass into ownership of the Priory on the death of their then owner, Richoard the Priest. The second or eastern group comprised St Nicholas in the Market and Holy Trinity, which should pass similarly after the death of the holder, a monk called Bristelm. Godfrey thought it possible that all these churches were in existence before the Conquest.[6] On the basis of these deeds a conjectural chart (Figure 5.2) has been compiled, showing the rise and fall of the parish churches.

In early borough rentals the parish of each property is frequently given, and is usually listed in any conveyance. Sometimes this is the only way of knowing where a property was situated, or gives a clue to where parish boundaries ran before the nineteenth-century maps were drawn. Confusion may arise where parishes have been merged and the property lies across the merged boundary, or where the property is in one parish but is also bounded on one side by another. An example in 1524 gives a meadow and garden in St Andrew's and All Saints parishes.[7] There was only a small length where the two had a boundary in common, at the southern end of Station Street, so the location can be fixed. Land similarly

CHURCH AND PARISH

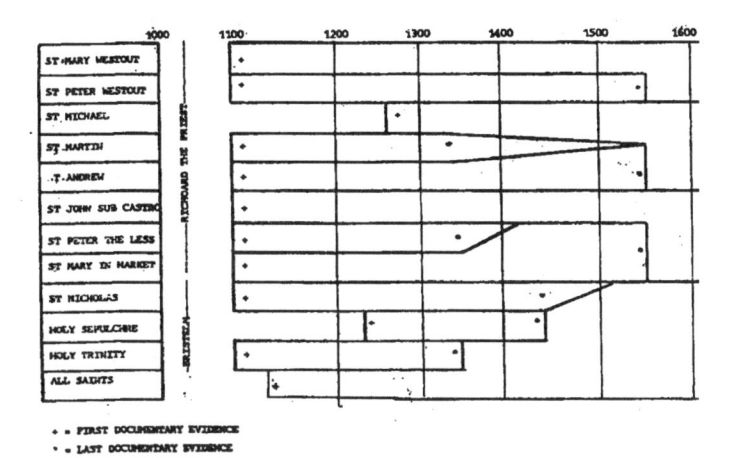

Figure 5.2. The growth and decline of the borough parishes.

described as in All Saints and St John in 1579 turns out merely to overlap the boundary.

St Michael, with St Andrew and St Martin

St Michael's church was not included in the 'western' group given to the Priory. It was probably held from the earliest times by the Archbishop of Canterbury, or the canons of Malling on his behalf, and was not in the gift of the de Warennes. It must have existed then, since the parishioners of St Andrew and St Martin had burial rights there. St Michael's is assumed to have been the mother church of these two, although the de Warennes held, and were able to give away their patronage of, the lesser ones.

The 1624 borough rental divided St Michael's into one part within and one part beyond the Westgate, and the western boundary of the 'inner' parish was the Anglo-Saxon defensive wall. At the end of the eighteenth century Dunvan wrote *'on the gradual decay of the fortification of this town, the wide*

Figure 5.3. St Michael's church, c.1880

ditch and rampart before the walls ... were made level and the ground so gained added to the parish of St Michael's which before had been limited by the western walls of the borough'.[8] Dunvan is not always accurate, but in this case there seems no good reason to doubt his main statement, and it fits the facts we know.[9] St Michael's later boundary crosses the High Street between Nos. 101 and 102 at the foot of St Anne's Hill, although from other information it has clearly moved about often. It passes along the gardens at the back of the YMCA and Women's Institute buildings in Westgate Street, and rejoins the town wall to the north at the beginning of New Road ('County Row' in 1824). From there it follows the castle wall anti-clockwise to the steps up from Castle Ditch Lane behind the law courts, where it rejoins what may have been the earliest line. From there it originally went south to include all the property up to the eastern edge of the present law courts (excluding the c.1900 eastwards extension). When the courts were built, the line moved further westwards to include the whole law courts. Crossing the High Street it goes down the western side of the cartway to the rear of the White Hart Hotel, and then more or less due south to the Winterbourne stream and the borough boundary, which it then follows westwards, before turning north beyond Keere Street.

St Michael's church is first named in a document of 1301 as lying in the patronage of the Prior and Chapter of Christchurch, Canterbury.[10] The Archbishop of Canterbury had a substantial presence in Lewes at Domesday, seven properties being held by the canons of St Michael of Malling, (within their manor of Stanmer) while he held twenty-one directly in Malling (later Ringmer) manor. Most of the frontage land near the church was later held of Lewes manor, but modern Nos. 86-7 are held by some unknown, outside manor, which could well be Malling, and has for many years had the name 'St Michael's House'. No other houses were identifiably held by the archbishop.

The northern arcade is of wood, and dates from the 1748 restoration *'when the parishioners could not attend divine service without great danger to their Lives'*. The arcade of the southern aisle of St Michael's Church is later than 1300 and suggests a rebuilding during the fourteenth century.[11] In fact the quality of the bricks supplied for this work was so poor that the churchwardens resolved to use squared, knapped flints instead, and thus have given to Lewes one of the finest, early examples of this technique.[12]

The sites of St Martin and St Andrew, the smaller churches now inside St Michael's parish, are lost. These would have been very small churches by modern standards, no more than the equivalent of private chapels of major land owners. Some burials may have taken place inside them. In 1488 A resident asked specifically in his will that he be buried in St Andrew's.[13] Number 73 High Street has been suggested as the site of St Martin's, and there is a good barrel-vaulted 'crypt' there, details of which have been dated to c.1100, but *'there is ... no reason to think that the chamber had an ecclesiastical connection'*.[14] St Martin's drops out of the records early, disappearing by 1316-17, being the first church to do so in the post-Conquest period. Its modest parochial resources continued to pay a pension to the Priory up to 1381, the smallest amount of any Lewes church.[15] By 1490, St Martin's Lane is described as being within the parish of St Andrew's.[16] St Michael's Lane has since vanished, although Bull Lane, (modern 'Paine's Twitten') probably represents the spinal road and lies in the correct relationship.

Opposite St Swithun's Lane is a lane running north, between Nos. 163 and 164, which has been pushed aside by the south western motte of the Castle. Now a private lane, it was at one time a public highway, closed only after a court case in 1877.[17] This line now runs clockwise around the motte ditch before exiting on the northern side, on Castle Lane, exactly where it would have if the lane had originally run straight across the site of the motte (Figure 5.4).

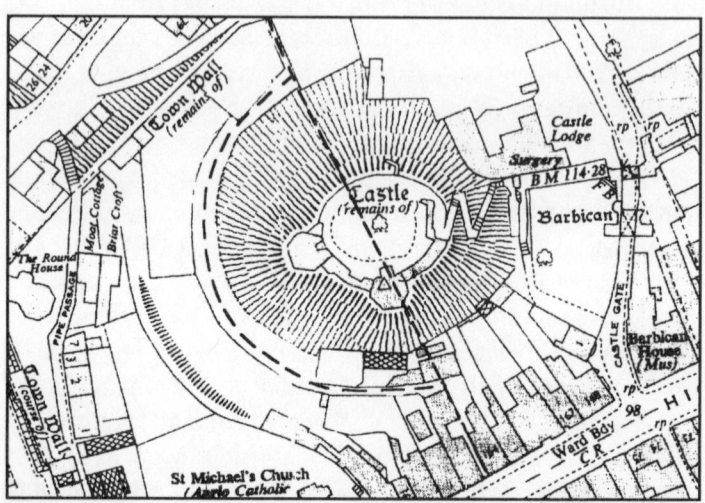

Figure 5.4. Private lane pushed aside by castle motte. Based on the 1967 Ordnance Survey 1:1250 map TQ4109 with the permission of The Controller of Her Majesty's Stationery Office, © Crown Copyright 87963M

St Andrew's parish can be seen to have been bounded to the north in 1478-9 by the Castle wall, which suggests that the Castle precinct was in existence by then.[18] St Andrew's was *'diminished and impoverished'* by 1337. A claim that fragmentary foundations found in the courtyard of Pelham House in St Andrew's Lane represented the church, was unfortunately not supported by evidence of interments or other identifiable religious remains.[19] William Figg refers to the demolition of remains of a church called 'St Mary Magdalene', which he identifies as St Mary in the Market, on the eastern side of Watergate Lane (corresponding now to No. 64 High Street) in 1856.[20] This mistake was instigated by Dunvan, who appears to have invented a (non-existent) church of St Mary Magdalene. This mistake may have originated from the will of George Wood of Selmeston, who died in 1691, which refers to a St Mary Magdalene, most likely to have been the chapel of St Mary Magdalene in St John the Baptist, Southover. If No. 64 High Street really was a church originally, then it was perhaps the site of St Andrew's, which continued in use until after the Dissolution.[21] At the Dissolution the crown retained the right of presentation and granted the Prior and Chapter of Canterbury a pension.

St John sub Castro, with the Chapel of Allington in St John Without, and the Churches of St Peter the Less and St Mary in the Market.

St John sub Castro parish had two dependent smaller churches and one chapel, and made up the remainder of Richoard the Priest's western group. It was in the gift of the de Warennes, so the whole modern parish can be called the mother parish. St John's is said to have been the earliest church in Lewes, and if the identification of lands before the Conquest in Frog Firle and Parrock as being in the possession of St John's is correct, then this is probably so.[22] In the apparent absence of any other identifiable pre-Conquest church of St John, then this one must have been the one referred to.

The parish was much larger originally, and has been divided in two by the insertion of Hamsey parish into Barcombe Hundred. This happened before the Conquest, and again argues a respectable antiquity for St John's. St John's in Lewes held and had confirmed to it during the eleventh century the chapel of Allington *'with the immunities and liberties which it has enjoyed from ancient times'*.[23] The two halves of the parish still exist, St John sub Castro having a common border with Hamsey to the north, while St John Without, now only a civil parish, lies mainly between Hamsey and East Chiltington, and still contains the site of the chapel of Allington (see Figure 5.5). In Lewes Borough, St John's

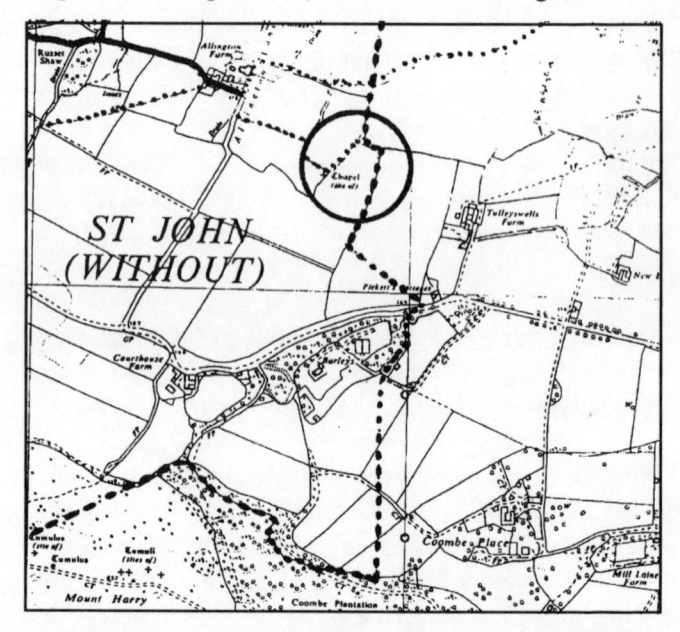

Figure 5.5. St John Without, showing site of chapel. Based on the 1961 Ordnance Survey 6" map TQ315E with the permission of The Controller of Her Majesty's Stationery Office, © *Crown Copyright 87963M*

boundary runs diagonally across the Paddock to the top end of Westgate Street, running with St Anne's, and there it briefly lines up with St Michael's. It continues along Castle Rise to Brack Mount, from there following the eastern side of the Castle wall clockwise around the Castle precinct to join with St Michael, with which it runs nearly to the end of Station Street. It stops before modern No. 18, then swings east and then north, mid-way between Station Street and St Nicholas' Lane to the eastern side of Nos. 45/6 High Street. It then continues northwards through the Corn Exchange of the Town Hall and north east to cross North Street at the exit to the modern car park. At the Town Hall and in North Street, parish boundary markers existed until 1874. At the car park, there is a marked change of direction towards the eastern end of Wellington Street, and then a further change as it crosses the Green Wall to run directly to the river, where it again turns northwards. This long tongue still stretches down Station Street and is the remains of the parish of St Mary in the Market. It is reasonable to suppose that the land north of the High Street was once the parish of St Peter the less. By 1381 St Peter no longer appears in the records as a Lewes church, having been dismantled around 1319, probably somewhere in the Fisher Street area.[24] There is a popular view that St Peter the Less is an early name for All Saints, but this cannot be sustained, for both churches are separately listed as far back as 1148.[25] In 1319 the pension it had previously paid to the Priory was given up and a substitute provided from the revenues of St John sub Castro, by then the parish church.[26]

St Peter the Less may have been so named to distinguish it from St Peter Westout, since no Saint called Peter 'the less' has been traced. The same pattern of 'greater' and 'less' church names appears in Chichester.[27] Much of the land in the parish was owned by the Priory of St Pancras, or by Malling (Ringmer) manor, and the whole parish identity is lost in the absence of records. The parish and the site of the church must therefore remain a matter for conjecture.

Figure 5.6. St John sub Castro.

St Mary's early parish was located in Station Street (once St Mary's Lane), with its eastern and western boundaries limited by St Michael and All Saints parishes. It became 'in foro' (in the Market) by 1255.[28] The church was 'demolished to the ground' in 1543-4, and its exact original location is not known.[29] Modern No. 49 High Street has been claimed as the site. This was for many years the 'Church House' of St Johns parish and was for a time the rectory, but it was always a burgage property of the borough manor and paid a secular quit-rent. Those who have interpreted a small piece of flintwork in the cellar of No. 49 as the remains of a church have vivid imaginations. It is also strange that most identifications of 'lost' churches occupy the sites of buildings on a north-south alignment, where one would expect to find an east-west aligned site. There is one more probable identification. Between 1498 and 1530 a series of grants (*'new rents'*) were being made along the High Street frontage opposite the Town Hall, a colonization of the previously open market place. Behind them a linked series of passages still represent an older frontage of the burgages between Station

Street and St Nicholas' Lane. We know that the church had a west door, and a belfry on the western end.[30] An anonymous manuscript relates how William Newman, who lived at No. 44 High Street (in All Saints parish) bought part of the garden of No. 45 (in St Mary's parish) and built a workshop on it.[31] In the process human remains were uncovered. These must represent burials inside the churchyard. Figure 5.7 shows this area, with the likely position of the workshop shown. This places the site of the church on the eastern edge of the old parish, some thirty feet behind the earlier frontage.

Early charters show land being conveyed by the Priory of St Pancras to various persons, and much of the eastern side of Station Street is later recorded as glebe land belonging to St

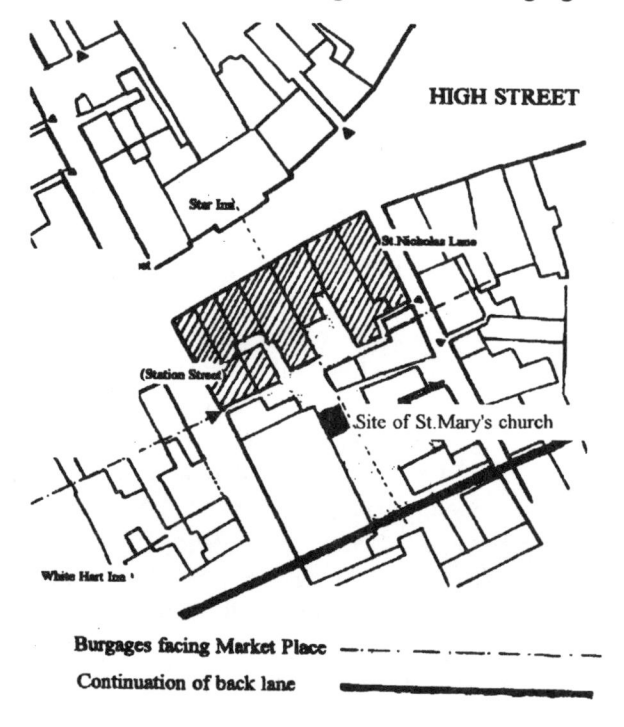

Figure 5.7. Forward encroachment by St Mary's parish.

Mary's or St John's parish. After absorbing the parish St Peter the Less sometime after 1319, St Mary's was in turn merged with St John sub Castro in 1538.[32]

All Saints, with St Nicholas', Holy Trinity, the Grey Friars and the Church of Holy Sepulchre

All Saints parish conveniently filled up the area between St John sub Castro and the river, except for a small part at the bottom of Station Street, which was originally in St Andrews, and still forms part of St Michael's. The 1337 proposals suggested that All Saints should take over the southern side of the High Street (School Hill), but in the event, it took over the whole of St Nicholas', St Sepulchre and Holy Trinity. The church is first named in 1148 in a confirmation by Pope Eugenius to Hilary, Bishop of Chichester.[33] Like St Michael's, it was not in any group given to the Priory, although it later took the position of mother church. It is tempting to see here evidence of some evolution of All Saints from a chapel serving the bishop's Lewes tenants.[34] All Saints was declared redundant before 1976, when a dedicated team of volunteers set out to rescue and preserve it for the town. It is now the property of the Town Council, and is a lively community youth and arts centre, (albeit perpetually if not chronically short of money). The earliest reference to the church is in 1148[35], but it is generally thought that the church was re-built during the fifteenth century after the amalgamation with St Sepulchre, Holy Trinity and St Nicholas.

All Saints churchyard was surrounded in the seventeenth century by an impressive stone wall, traces of which remain, particularly on its northern side.[36] The church had then the same shape as that shown in the picture in the Sharpe Collection at Michelham Priory. Broomans Lane and Church Lane there joined and ran together into the High Street, contrary to the arrangement found now. A cottage to the east

Figure 5.8. Broomans Lane and All Saints, from Randoll's map, c. 1620.

was bounded on its northern and eastern sides by a *'little way from the Church Way to the water called the Hair Ditch'*.[37] So there were then Broomans and Church Lanes, and the little way to the Hair Ditch, which may be an alternative name for Pinwell Lane.

Many entries in the register of the Bishops of Chichester refer to *'The Church of Lewes'*. It is not unnatural for the bishop to refer to All Saints, the only church to which he had original title, in this way. Convocations of Lewes and Pevensey Deaneries were also held there, and novices from the nearby Grey Friars ordained. The fifteenth-century building is illustrated in the Sharpe Collection (Nos. 204 and 206a), when it had the present tower, a conventional nave with chancel and a small north chapel. On the southern side of the nave there is shown a two-storey porch of which nothing is now known, but it may have had a schoolroom on the upper floor. All of this was demolished in 1806/7, when a Georgian preaching nave with a small eastern apsidal end was built.

Whilst repairing the leadwork of the tower recently, a plaque of signatures was found, listing 'A. H.Wilds', but with the 's' scratched off as though to make it 'Wild'. It was A. H.Wilds' father Amon Wilds (1762-1833) who rebuilt the church, demolishing all but the tower and adding the preaching nave. Perhaps A. H.Wilds was occupied in stitching together the old tower and the new nave. He would have been twenty-two in 1807, and only began to achieve real prominence in his later work in Brighton, particularly after 1823, when he joined the firm of C. H. Busby. Beneath the inscription are the names T. and D. Ade, along with the date 1807. (I am indebted to Mr Mike Helps for this information.) The Ades were churchwardens at the time. They were also coachbuilders, their business premises being at No. 34 High Street, in the parish.

In the disused chancel, behind the mirror panelling at the eastern end, is a substantial mosaic by Salviati of Milan, depicting the Last Supper. On the southern wall of the nave are parts of a memorial to Jane Stansfield, grandmother of John Evelyn the diarist and arboriculturalist, and John Stansfield, her second husband. The cast-iron columns of the balcony are founded directly on the walls of the old church, giving an idea of its size. The chancel did not extend further east than the middle of the stage area.

St Nicholas 'in foro' was merged with All Saints, despite the fact that it functioned as the market church. Its western parish boundary was in common with St Mary in the Market, but there is nothing to show where its eastern boundary was. I have suggested that the western boundary ran up to the marker at the entrance to the North Street car park, and then returned along my proposed line of the Anglo-Saxon wall. The church stood about where the War Memorial is now, and was unique in that was located in the middle of the street, in the market

Figure 5.9. All Saints, Lewes. Lambert.

place at the top of School Hill. This was a common situation for the market church in other towns. After 1319 it was *'in ruins'* and from that date on declined further, although it seems to have still been roofed, and the tower still standing, in 1620.[38] It was not included in a list of churches surrendered at the Dissolution, having been converted to secular use before then, and its title as the market church was taken over by St Mary (Blessed Mary in the Market) from the mid-fourteenth century.[39]

St Nicholas' had a chequered secular career as the 'Broken Church', and in 1571 the constables and Fellowship took the lease of a piece of waste ground inside its walls, to let at a profit rent in order to help meet the town charges. This part of its history is well documented, but there is more information to be obtained from an examination of the area covered by the parish. The ruined building stood until 1761, when it was demolished and a new market house built in what is now called Market Street.

With few exceptions, nearly all the land which lay inside St Nicholas' parish was held by the manor of Southover. It is to be expected that this area, in the bustling heart of the town, would have been coveted by the Priory, which was still presenting to the living in 1410, although the church had long been derelict.

Little is known of Holy Trinity, now part of All Saints parish. By 1319 the church was said to have been entirely ruined by storms and gales, but despite the revision of church boundaries, in 1381 it was still paying a pension to the precentor of the Priory.[40] Its eastern boundary seems reasonably securely located at the river, but the western boundary is lost. It has attracted much comment, beginning with Dunvan and ending with the last 'official' guide to Lewes, where in both cases it is confidently asserted that it remains visible in the cellars of No. 214 High Street. I looked there carefully in 1972 and found nothing to indicate an early building of any appropriate age, ecclesiastical or not.[41] The idea mainly arises from the Latin description in 1624 of a property near there as *'nuper domus ecclesie'*.[42] This merely means 'lately the church house', and in any case refers to No. 213. There were other 'church houses' in Lewes (e.g. St John's and St Anne's), let out as burgage properties to provide a rent income. This one like the others paid the secular quit-rent.

If little is known about Holy Trinity, then even less is known of Holy Sepulchre. It certainly existed, it was somewhere in what is now All Saints, but it was *'decayed'* in 1319, and in the 1337 re-arrangements, it and the parishioners were provided for in the apportionment between St John's and All Saints. After the church had gone, the parish still existed, as late as 1432.[41] The dedication is that of a church of the Knights Templar. Their order was established in 1119, and their first English house two years later. A date of about 1150 for the Lewes church could be expected, but the first evidence is a 1237 conveyance of property in the parish in the High Street, given by Philip the Chaplain of Balsdean and Vicar of

CHURCH AND PARISH

Rottingdean.[44]

The Turk's Head may have had its origin as St Sepulchre church. Randoll's Map shows an L-shaped building with a wall fronting the High Street, a doorway through the wall, and open space on either side, that to the west bounded by a wall. John Luck (or Tuck) was an innkeeper who occupied the Turk's Head Inn in 1683. A later owner was Samuel Wheatley, but by 1765 his daughters had closed the inn and sold the premises to Dr John Barham, Doctor of Physick.

William de Warenne III went on a Crusade in 1147 and died two years later. A possible scenario could be that the next generation of de Warennes set aside some of their demesne land of Houndean manor in the town for the erection of a Templar church, as a pious act of remembrance for the dead earl. In 1337 John de Bourne, a Templar, was a confessor to the family.[45] From later rentals part of the parish is seen to be held of Houndean manor and not of the borough. There is a

Figure 5.10. Turk's Head, from Randoll's map, c. 1620.

popular but fallacious belief that all Templar churches were circular. Such a shape was very rare and only ten are known to have been built during the twelfth century. Only six of these are Templar. However, since we do not know whether Holy Sepulchre in Lewes was round, square, oblong or any other shape, and cannot be certain where it was, we can only hope for some further evidence to emerge. In the passageway leading from the back of No. 210 High Street northwards behind Albion House there are dressed stone blocks in the western wall, some of which may have details dating from that period.[46]

Most of the land between the Bridge and Friars Walk (except for the town wharf) was occupied by the Convent of St Mary of the Friars Minor, generally known as the Grey Friars. Rowe refers to it as a *'supposed liberty'* because it was crown land in his time, and tenants there claimed to be exempt from service to the town, although their claims do not seem to have succeeded. Mr Mark Gardiner's report of the recent excavations is now published, but this deals with the archaeology of the site, and it would be wrong to interpret too much history from this. He claims that the site would have been a hard for beaching boats before the Friars settled there.[47]

The Franciscans came to England in 1224 and by 1237 were established in Chichester, and in Lewes by 1241.[48] As was consistent with their vows, they occupied low-lying land beside the river terrace and the causeway to the river-crossing and bridge. In a will of 1524 it is described as the church of St Francis of the Friars Minor, and a chapel of St Barbara is mentioned, but according to the Victoria County History (Vol. Seven) the correct dedication was *'St Mary and St Margaret'*.

The land called Southover had been given to the Priory of St Pancras, and Southover parish included all the land on the southern side of Friars Walk and Lansdown Place, except for a narrow strip to the south and east, which was waste of the borough. Randoll's Map does not show the strange 'salient' caused by the diversion of the borough boundary round the Grey Friars, but Deward's map does. William de Warenne I assured the Priory that if he or his successors established any new religious foundation, it would be placed under the control of St Pancras.[49] How the Grey Friars obtained the original grant of land is therefore not known, but it is possible that by that time, Hameline de Warenne, (natural son of Count Henry of Anjou, and half brother to Henry II) did not regard himself as bound by any undertaking of his wife's great grandfather. The Friars had access to tithes, much of which were in the de Warenne demesne manors, particularly in Houndean.[50] It may be relevant that the foundation of the Grey Friars at Winchelsea is thought to have been acheived by a royal charter and not by the bishop or archbishop.[51]

Of the western side by Friars Walk, Gideon Mantell (b.1789) wrote in his youth of *'A high bank which served as a footpath on the eastern side of the road, abutted against the [Friars] Wall'.*[52] The name Friars Wall seems to have been changed to Friars Walk when the stones of the wall were taken to adorn the front of Dial House, Nos. 220-1 High Street. Again, according to the maps, the Friars Wall enclosed the western and northern sides of the precinct, with a gateway and a pair of small houses beside them, probably about where Fitzroy House now stands.

In 1538 the Friars were suppressed, and in 1541 the site and buildings were leased for twenty-one years to Sir John Gage.[53] Three years later, William Heydon and Hugh Stuckley, acting as agents for the crown, sold the reversion of John Gage's lease to John Keyme.[54] John Kyme was an interesting Lewesian who has had little previous attention. His father was also John Kyme (or Cayme, or Keyme), a trustee of the Lewes Free School in 1512, who died in about 1548, in some poverty. His son obtained much property in Lewes, but as he was without direct heirs these holdings passed through his brothers and sisters, particularly through his sister Katherine (d. 1564),

Figure 5.11. The Friars by Lambert, 1777, showing buildings near the town wharf.

who married John Awcock. Their descendants (after a spelling shift to Alcocke) inherited the 'Greyfriars'. Kyme was Steward to Sir William Petre, Secretary to Henry VIII and the next three monarchs. He served from 1536 throughout the period of monastic dissolution. He was involved in the dissolution of The Priory of St Pancras, and it was small wonder that in the process he picked up the small Grey Friars and some other ecclesiastical property in his home town. There was nothing improper in this, at least by the mores of the time.

As Petre's senior household officer, he maintained his master's accounts. He appears to have been thorough, careful and scrupulous. It is a pity that we do not have more of his own papers to flesh out his story. He left Petre's employment after 1562, before Petre himself died, in 1572, at his principal house at Ingatestone in Essex. Kyme would by then have had possession by reversion of the site. He lived there until 1585, and on his death that year he was buried in All Saints church. Whether what we see in Randoll's 1620 Map is the old Friary building, or a house that Keyme built on the site, is still problematical.[55] What seems certain from the maps is that what was shown on the 1624 map was still there in 1824. It looks Elizabethan. It had a hall, parlour, great chamber, a chamber over the parlour, a kitchen with a chamber over it, and a further chamber. It was probably about the same size as Anne of Cleves House. The map elevations of the house depict a substantial long range, with two gabled crosswings on an east-west axis, and the same orientation and shape of building appears on later maps. Figg's map of 1775 also shows a conjectural chapel in a location which seems not to have been covered by the recent excavation.

Between Keyme's house and the High Street there was built the house known as 'The Friars', a separate building. The old house was inherited by Susanna Alcocke, and she and her husband Thomas Pellatt probably built the new one. It bore a foundation stone dated 1673.[56] This house descended into the ownership of the Pellatts until Apsley Pellatt III sold it to George Verrall in 1803. By this time it was usually let to tenants. A nineteenth-century painting by James Lambert shows this later house, and just beyond it a glimpse of what may be the older house.[57]

Verrall broke up the estate, but sold the house to Nehemiah Wimble, who entertained King William IV and Queen Adelaide here in 1830. There is a large commemorative oil painting of the occasion which hangs in the Assembly Room of the Town Hall. The painting (if cleaned) would clearly show classical architecture of the later seventeenth century, and thus denies its attribution by other writers to the Tudor period.

Chapter Six
The Market

As we have seen, long before the Norman Conquest, a market had come into being in Lewes. It could even be that the market came first, the burh afterwards. Certainly, like the borough, the market was 'prescriptive', and it was so described in a Local Act of Parliament in 1791.[1] This argues a long history. Burhs established around the time of King Alfred were conceived as centres of trade as well as of defence. The king's burh enjoyed the king's special peace, and on market days its influence would have extended further. The actual limit may have been about five miles, determined by the time taken to reach the marketplace, and to return home afterwards, in the course of a day. Perhaps this distance seems a little short if you were selling small portable items, but try driving a few pigs to market and see how long it takes to cover five miles! Pigs, like Sussex people, 'won't be druv'. Inside the king's special peace, people could come and go at will. Once they were within the town walls they could meet at road junctions, and do business. The laws of the time ensured that buying and selling could only occur at a properly appointed market, in the presence of witnesses. So if someone claimed that your horse was his horse, the market witnesses would have to testify and decide. As the flow of trade increased, so the area in which the market was conducted became formalised, and traders lived in the town, and had booths which they erected on market days. Traders found it to their advantage to buy burgage property, particularly where it faced onto the market place. This is why the burgages in the market area commanded twice the normal quit-rent. Market laws insisted that all deals should be done during daylight, in the open air, and the ability to store goods close to the point of sale made these plots the most attractive. The market witnesses later became the officers of the market.

THE MARKET

In some larger market towns, groups of traders in the same trade formed their own specialist market in areas close to the main centre. Lewes was a small town, and with the possible exception of the fishmongers, who congregated on the southern side of the High Street west of St Martin's Lane, and the wool merchants who were in the best position on the northern side, east of Castlegate, there is little other evidence for these smaller groupings of traders.

Trading in the presence of witnesses was a formal, legal requirement. Until a markethouse was established there would always have been a problem in finding witnesses when you wanted them. The market court house provided a place where market officers could be found and do their work. The laws stated that, in hundreds or in small burhs, twelve official witnesses should be appointed. Twelve witnesses became the Market Court, and in Lewes provided the basis of the Merchant Gild, and the Society of Twelve. In Saxon times '... *wohsceapung'* (fines for buying or selling contrary to the rules of the market), could be collected in the market, and disposed of as gifts, or let to farm.[2]

Those who traded in the market were expected to compensate the king for the advantages provided. *'... the Boroughs were a haven for merchants. Trade was deliberately channelled through them, and all housed one or more mints.*[3] Also provided were approved sets of weights and measures. No one was allowed to coin money except in a burh, and the moneyer used approved royal dies (for which he had to pay). Every burh had its moneyer, and Lewes was no exception. Some extra importance has been claimed for Lewes because it is recorded as having two moneyers while Chichester had only one. However, Lewes had only one mint and as to the two moneyers, it is likely that one was old and on the edge of retirement. Banking as we now know it has evolved only over the last 200-250 years and so is a relatively recent function, yet the store of value had to exist in some way before this. There must have been persons who performed banking functions, in the time between the early moneyers and the later joint-stock bankers. All those trading in the market would be expected to pay money to the king, or later to the manor, for the privilege and the convenience of doing business there. That money constituted the market 'toll' which was an important element in the town's finances.

The market place in Lewes was not a fixed and immutable area. It grew up around the 'Star Corner' crossroads of the High Street, Fisher Street and St Mary's Lane. It was at this point that the quit-rents and ownerships of property are at their most confused, evidence for the relative antiquity of the area. The booths outside the burgage tenements actually became fixtures, and many tenements crept forward to absorb their associated booth area. For better protection an upper floor was built, and the absorbed booth became part of the house, followed by the erection of a new, detached booth, and a repeat of the whole process. In 1617 Daniel Rickman was fined one shilling, with a further ten shillings payable if he failed to remove a shop he had erected in front of his tenement in the High Street.[4]

From shortly after the foundation of the Priory of St Pancras, the de Warennes were granting the right of pre-emption of what was available at the market, to the Priory. They had the right, but only after the lords of the barony and their heirs, to the market of logs on Tuesdays, Thursdays and Saturdays from Whitsun to Lammas, and this was extended in c.1190 for *'so long as carriage continues'*. They also had pre-emption, under the same restrictions, of rights to the markets of flesh and fish, whether at Lewes or Seaford, or anywhere else. This confirms that a market existed in Lewes from at least 1089.[5]

There were two 'murages', or taxes on the market to raise money for building and repairing the walls of the town. The first was raised in 1266, after some delay caused by the Battle of Lewes, until the Battle of Evesham had restored the status quo. It was directed to the *'Good Men'* of Lewes towards enclosing the town with walls. The de Warennes maintained overall control, and in 1268 freed the abbot and convent of Hide Abbey (in Winchester) and their men of Southease and Telscombe, of all exactions and demands for an enclosing wall in the vill of Lewes.[6] Although all other records of it are now lost, this suggests that Hide Abbey did own land in Lewes at the time.

The line of these walls could well have followed parts of the earlier Anglo-Saxon defences, but it is more likely that they would have recognised the subsequent expansion of the town. This fact may account for persistent, later claims that the original town walls ran around the lower edges of the town rather than on the higher ground, and the possible move of the Eastgate from its defensive position near the top of School Hill, to an administrative, market-led position at its foot.

Whether the goods listed in the murage tax records were a survey of what was actually traded in the market, or a conventional 'likely' list is uncertain. In the 1266 murage nothing unexpected is mentioned (except possibly for a tax on squirrels), and many items being traded coincide with those listed in later records. The second murage tax was raised in 1334, sixty years after the Battle of Lewes, and perhaps only the items which differ from those in the earlier list are significant. Why a second murage should have been necessary so soon is not clear, although it does seem to have occurred around the time the Barbican Gate of the Castle was constructed. Goats appear, as well as sheep and hogs, and pewter has been added to tin. Many metals and metal products were now being traded, suggesting that the Wealden metal-working industry was developing. Firewood, charcoal, nails, horseshoes, clouts and steel rods are all ironworking goods, and also listed are brass, copper, alum, copperas, argot (a form of sliver) and verdigris. Lampreys were taxable before Easter, and the trade in squirrel pelts was mentioned along with lamb, kid, hare, rabbit, fox and cat skins. Sea fish (mentioned in 1266) and fresh or salt salmon (mentioned in 1334) are good evidence for maritime trade, and a tax on *'Barges with things for sale'* may represent the earliest evidence for river-borne trade.

The market for sheep, cattle and horses was important and long lasting. Trade in horses and oxen appears in the Domesday Book, and by the middle of the nineteenth century, was still being held on alternate Tuesdays. The area used was the High Street, from the White Hart Inn westwards towards St Michael's church.[7] Writing from personal recollection, a High Street resident recorded that the wattle pens took up a great part of the width of the road and interfered a good deal with the other traffic.[8] About this time, names from earlier documents can tell us about the trades of Lewes and its inhabitants, although mobility had already begun to destroy the continuity of names and occupations. In 1340 parliament granted the king a subsidy, representing one-ninth of the value of the goods of (among others) residents and traders in the boroughs. The actual amounts are not germane to this study, but the relative values and names are of use. Thus Julian Combere, William le Frye and John Sire were the highest taxed, followed by Henry Sadlere, Thomas Coupere, William More, and one illegible. Next in descending order came Agnes Barnard and Simon Orloger, and then William Cartere, John Wekere and William Fisschere. Of these names, Tannere, Cartere, Bakere, Bochere, Orloger, Combere, Fisschere, Sadlere, Coupere and Spicer, represent trades, although it is by no means certain that these individuals still practised them. In the 1377-8 Poll Tax on 150 male and female residents, (but not including wives of males) there were six wool merchants, six clothiers, four hosiers, a spicer, eight butchers, three bakers, three cobblers and two smiths.[9] Robert Drapere was a cloth merchant, William Bochere was a butcher, Walter and William Ferour were smiths, but John and William Cotillar (Cutler) were also butchers. Other names of occupation can be seen, but not positively identified as carrying on their trades. Such were Peyntour, Bakere, Spycer, Chapman, Taillour,

Messager, Roper, Gardyner, Helyer (Healier or roofer), Brasyere, Shyppman, Tornour, Boteller, Clerke, Barbour, Carter, Sherman (Shearman or wool-shearer) and Glovere.

In 1524-5, Subsidy Rolls give some idea of relative wealth, not only of individuals but of parts of the town. In St Mary Westout Peter Flussher was by far and away the wealthiest resident, but otherwise the wealthy seem to have lived in St Michael's, including Emma Smyth, Joan Holter (widow), Thomas Smyth, John Ivye and John Cotmot, while further down were Daniel Mariet, John Holter, John Holter Jr., Emma, Elizabeth and William Holter. Put together, the Holter family were wealthy and powerful. Very few of these names represent trades, and where there is a trade the Subsidy Roll often makes a point in many cases of stating the relevant trade name, e.g. Cornellus the Mason, John Lees (scythemaker), Gaskyn Hacford or hatmaker, Cornellus the baker. These Rolls list many Lewes residents as 'aliens', persons who were *'attracted to England because of the persistence of conditions disturbing for the ordinary people of western Europe'.*[10] Some of them were by then as wealthy as the native burgesses. For example Hans Legate, Harman Cowper, and John Petersen were financially able to look their fellow citizens in the face. Most of their original surnames caused difficulty and sometimes had to be Anglicised. Many of them appear regularly in later documents as established surnames in the property ownerships of the town. Herman Glasier, Harman Couper, Han Paynter, Cornellus the mason, Robert Berchir the 'Doucheman', Charles Capper and Gaskyn Hatmaker were just a random selection from the lists. German Hardiman was a prominent citizen of the later sixteenth century, and served as senior constable. Perhaps Benjamin, John and Thomas Harman (a name still found in Lewes) were relatives who had shortened the name. They also served as constables or as members of the Fellowship.

The emphasis on the cloth trade indicates a specialisation for which Lewes seemed to have a high reputation in the thirteenth century. In what has been described as *'surely the product of an idle hour'*, a well-travelled merchant listed the products he associated with various settlements all over England. Not all were complimentary, some towns being famous (in his judgement) for prostitutes, thieves or murderers, but Lewes was listed as being famous for wimples, the elaborate headwear of ladies of the time.[11] The author's closing note was:

> *There's plenty of places*
> *But too much to drink*
> *And much more to say*
> *but my wits are away.*

One must have some sympathy with him. Robert le Wympler is listed as a witness in the chartulary of the Priory of St Pancras, in a context that relates to this period.[12] Chichester was listed for its beggars, and Rye for merling (fish), but, sadly, no other towns in Sussex are mentioned.

During the sixteenth and seventeenth centuries the officers appointed to control the market had descriptive titles.[13] There were clerks of the corn or grain market, a fish market, a butchery (earlier known as the flesh market), a cloth market (called the wool market in 1588), to which was added the market of spars and withes. The cloth market was so named in 1614 and 1616. The extent of their jurisdiction seems to have been limited. In 1649 the constables presented to the Easter Sessions *'upon the severall complaints of the inhabitants of Lewis Millars who take much more toll in these deere times then is their due'.* Among the other, less important officers were a pinder (pound keeper), searcher and sealer of leather (both a function of the lords of the borough), scavenger, and ale connors or tasters, one for each of the four parishes.

It is interesting (if puzzling) to note that in 1613, William James, the clerk of the butchery, presents to the court the fact that he killed a bull and a pig, contrary to the regulations, and was thus fined one shilling. In most cases an offence of this kind involved killing pregnant animals, so it is difficult to see how this can apply to a bull. James was clearly making a statement of some sort!

Where there was an offence against the manor, the market clerks were seemingly more precise. This applied particularly to the offence of selling improperly tanned hides, when both the searcher as well as the sealer of leather were called into action. They had then to empannel a group of six 'leathermen' to pass judgement. One only sees in the record when a prosecution was successful, and there may have been cases where the seller was found not to be at fault. In most cases, where a fine was levied, it was of the order of seven to ten shillings, of which one-third belonged to the lords of the manor, with confiscation of the offending hide. In 1620 Salomon Minge of Wivelsfield (which gives an idea of the area over which Lewes market could 'pull' custom) was in breach of the code, but only for the butt and the neck of his hide, so he was fined only four shillings for those defective parts, and presumably allowed to keep the balance.

All of these officers carried out their functions from the market house, or at least did so when it was built. In 1564 a Mrs Holter (presumably the widow of the prominent Lewes butcher of that name) gave ten pounds towards the building of a Market House, which the constables and other citizens voluntarily increased by another ten pounds. Nineteen pounds and five shillings was finally spent, the surplus being returned proportionately to the subscribers after its building in 1565. This was the small circular or octagonal building shown in Randoll's 1620 Map of Lewes, situated at the mouth of Castlegate. It appears to have been not dissimilar to the equivalent building at Chichester, but on a much smaller scale. Godfrey gave a full account of the subject, the following being a summary of his work.[14] That building survived until 1648-9 when *'In this yeare the old market howse was pulled down in*

Saint Michaell parish & ye newe set up in ye roome'.[15] In that year the market experienced problems, seemingly caused by the amount of space it was taking up. The Earl of Dorset wrote to the civic leaders in an attempt to put an end to the controversy, saying that he preferred that the corn market should be kept in the place where it always had been, but if this proved to be too small they could use waste land held by him in his part of the manor.[16] Despite this gesture the Market House remained in the same location, although by now in a new building, where it stayed until 1792. The little round market house disappeared. No representation of the second market house has come down to us, but there is a view looking up to the castle barbican which suggests that it may have been on the site of No. 168 High Street.[17]

In 1789, at an adjourned Lawday, the inhabitants resolved to set up a committee to fix on a proper spot of ground to erect a market house. The committee met shortly after and considered the Castle Yard, on the land now occupied by Castle Lodge, but at that time part of the ground of the Castle Inn, or land adjoining that held by Lord Hampden in St John sub Castro near the Star Inn, or land owned by Mr W. B. Langridge in All Saints. The decision was not unanimous, a minority favouring the Castle site. The committee eventually decided, in favour of the minority, to take the land in the Castle Yard, and set about measuring it (the building to be 108 feet long and 50 feet wide, the cost to be £450). They also proposed applying for an Act of Parliament to obtain a charter for the market to replace the prescriptive market. They then set about raising the money. The lords of the manor had their interest protected by allowing them the right to appoint the clerk. What followed next is hidden deep inside the town records. The committee adjourned to 12 October, but seems to have been unable to meet until the 23rd, when it received an answer from the lords of the borough, and hastily adjourned itself until 23 November 1790. There seems to have been a lot of paddling in murky waters, resulting in a meeting in August 1791 in which, without further reference to the lands in the Castle, it was resolved to build the new market on the grounds of Lord Hampden. It seems that the lords of the borough decided to resist the idea of using the Castle precinct, and effectively vetoed the original proposal. So in 1791 proposals were made for a new market house to be built on Lord Hampden's land, where the Market Tower is now. The work was carried out by by Amon Wilds (senior) with others, and opened in 1792. The building survives to this day.[18] The new market was taken out of the hands of the old clerks of the market, and was newly constituted by local Act of Parliament under market commissioners.[19] William Lee's outburst in 1799 (see Chapter Four) led for a while to George Grantham being appointed, in what could only have been an honorific task, as a sort of Pooh-bah, occupying all the offices of the market and being ale conner for all four parishes. Originally the market tower stood alone, but in 1808 an extension was built on its southwestern side and let as a shop. In 1872, when the tower passed into the ownership of the borough council, this and another shop on the other side of the tower were converted into offices. These are still there, although one was for a time converted into a public lavatory.

The building specification refers to *'... the reception of a certain bell formerly belonging to the broken church of St Nicholas ... and of a clock to strike on the said bell'*.[20] In 1786 the bell had been deposited in the lower court of the Sessions House and the clock was being stored in a stable owned by Henry Humphrey, at Lewes House. The bell is called 'Old Gabriel', around which grew up a strange superstition that it was only rung on occasions of great importance. 'Old Gabriel', as it is known from the inscription *gabrielis menti dedus habio nomen,* is the largest pre-Reformation bell in the county, and was cast by John Tonne (a Frenchman) before 1536.[21]

Recently the clock mechanism has been restored and rings out the hours. For those who have heard it this is not the voice of Old Gabriel, but the bell of the clock. It is recorded in

1800 that *'The Market Clock [that was] is in the late erected building adjoining St Michael's church'*, while Gabriel and another old clock were in the town tower. So the 'market' clock which had originally been in the market house seems to have been that then (and now) in St Michael's. While the first market house may have contained this clock, it does appear, from Randoll's Map, to have been quite small, and is therefore unlikely to have had one. Even so, the market cross in Chichester, with its clock, presented a challenge to Lewes's civic pride, and the subject still has some mileage in it.

The workings of the market at this time appear in the records of the View of Frankpledge because the View was still the court authorised to deal with offences. It is an indication either of health, or perhaps indifference, that in many years the clerks of the separate markets present that 'everything is well'.

No market can exist without access to money. For many years title to a property, with income arising from it, was the only alternative to a pot of gold in the back bedroom, as a means of storing wealth. For this reason, properties in Lewes High Street were continually changing hands and debts were being incurred on them. The earliest bankers may have been the king's moneyers, and goldsmiths, who by the nature of their work had to occupy secure premises, acting as custodians for individual 'liquid' fortunes. Even so it must have been a very cumbersome system, and by the end of the eighteenth century the forerunners of the present joint-stock banks were beginning to appear. By about 1753, Thomas Harben (in association with Thomas Dicker) was the first such banker in Lewes, although I cannot identify his premises earlier than 1790, when he was at No. 174-5 High Street.[22] This was only a few years before he over-extended himself and his banking operations failed. Harben was a wealthy man but most of his assets were tied up in land.

Harben called his new bank, founded in 1789, the 'Lewes Old Bank', presumably as there was merit in being the first bank established in Lewes. By 1793 he had moved into the eastern part of what was then Newcastle House at No. 182 High Street, but by 1796 he was forced to sell out to Molineux and Whitfield, and the 'New Bank' took over. The original partners were Joseph Molineux, an ironmonger, Francis Whitfield, a woolstapler, with Benjamin Comber, a goldsmith who also described himself as a banker as far back as 1771, and Richard King, a soap boiler and tallow chandler. Comber and King dropped out by 1806. Their banking activities were carried out originally from Richard King's house, at No. 190 High Street, and on taking over Harben's bank they closed down his offices in Newcastle House. There were many permutations of name until 1896, when the partnership was taken over by Barclay and Company, continuing to the present day as Barclays Bank, the 'Lewes Old Bank'.

On the principle that people come to a town for one purpose, and make use of other facilities when there, doctors soon recognised the value of being associated with a prosperous market. There were many medical doctors in Lewes, beginning with barber-surgeon Thomas Blunt in 1611. John Panton, Thomas Fissenden, Richard Godman and Benjamin White were particularly prominent in the seventeenth century. John Holney, the Russell family, John Turner, John Snashall, Joseph Ridge and Thomas Frewen all had a high reputation during the eighteenth. Although Dr John Tabor (the antiquarian researcher of the Roman villa at Eastbourne) lived in Lewes then, and was undoubtedly a doctor of medicine (physick) there is no evidence for his having practiced. Surgeons appear at the end of the eighteenth century, among them Dr David Bayford and James Moore. Gideon Mantell and Avery Roberts appear in the nineteenth. The John Turner of 1749 (No. 17 High Street) founded a dynasty, with Richard Turner appearing there in 1871, and the partnership of Turner, Crosskey and Dow by 1898.

Chapter Seven
Westout and Without

Westout and Without have been given little attention in the past, and so have a claim to a chapter on their own. Although the churches of St Peter and St Mary Westout held land in separate ownership, the territory eventually became totally muddled.

In William de Warenne II's grant, St Peter and St Mary are described as *'In Westute two churches with their appurtenances ... with two messuages and the land of Aldewalle.'* The two messuages are presumably parsonage houses, and the land of Aldewalle must surely be what we know as the Wallands. The churches were given by the de Warennes to the Priory, but Westout retained its' separation from Southover and from Lewes by remaining part of Swanborough Hundred. In 1538, because of the poverty of St Peter's, the Bishop of Chichester decreed that the churches, incumbents, parishioners and revenues of St Peter and St Mary were to be united.

St Peter Westout

For St Peter it is possible to maintain some separation in the records, for it was an urban parish. The church was perhaps informally known as the Greater, in contrast to St Peter the Less in the old borough. In common with so many other towns, the parish represents the more fashionable, westwards extra-urban development of the borough beyond the original burh. The site of the church, now beneath No. 110 High Street, is reasonably certain. It was disbanded in 1537, and dismantled thereafter. In 1600 the rector held a garden *'south of his rectory and west of the cemetery of St Peters',* by copyhold of the borough manor.[1]

WESTOUT AND WITHOUT

Figure 7.1. "Old church of St Peter Westout, now used as outhouse to the Boarding School in St Annes, Lewes, by Lambert Senr, in 1773."

This shows that he was using property here as a rectory. It is difficult to see anything church-like in the illustration in Horsfield's *History of Lewes* of 1773, when the rectory was said to still be in existence.[2] In 1790 the rector of St Anne's was holding the old church, but on the same spot Widow Luxford had a property *'late of Miss Lund'*, and Miss Ryall held another. Both ladies had run schools at this location.[3] Perhaps what is shown are premises on the street frontage used as a school, and not the church itself. Masonry remains of the church were found during the digging of foundations for the new rectory that still stands on the site. Some of these found their way into the wall on the southern side of Rotten Row, and can still be seen.[4]

St Anne's Hill passes through the parish, otherwise the only other streets were Rotten Row, which curved down the southern side to the bottom of Winterbourne Hollow, and a lateral lane going southwards into Southover over St Pancras Bridge, now St Pancras Road. Land on the northern side of St Anne's Hill was held by Houndean manor, except for a few burgage tenement holdings of the borough. Antioch street, which ran parallel to, and some distance west of, Keere Street, may once have been the western edge of the old borough outside the town walls, but after it had gone, the boundary tended to move about. St Michael's, outside the borough at this point, still existed in the seventeenth century.

The first houses on the southern side of the street were Nos. 102 and 103. Antioch House (No. 104) was held by Thomas Sherman in 1597 as a tenement and garden *'lying outside the Westgate of Lewes Town'* of the manor of Plumpton.[5] He also held another house belonging to Plumpton Manor, sometime Bryans, now No. 105 High Street, which could have been part of the same property.[6]

A tenement called Rotten Row held by the widow of Slutter, appears c. 1570 for fourpence rent.[7] Four houses in Rotten Row were given by Richard Rykehurst in 1586, *'lyinge on the back side of St Peter's Church'*, and in 1624 were held by William Inyans, Rector of St Anne's, again *'once Slutters'* and for fourpence rent. Dr John Slutter was the stipendiary curate of St Michael's church in 1556.[8] Three of the houses were to be used for the accomodation of poor people, and one let to produce an income to maintain the others. As with so many other charitable acts in Lewes, the trustees were dilatory and the property was neglected. It has been assumed that it was for this reason they became Rotten Row, but the name existed before 1570, i.e. before Rykehurst's gift. In 1557, what was probably the same land, but not then named 'Rotten Row', was conveyed to trustees by Thomas Slutter as free land with barns and gardens, late in the parish of St Peter and now *'... in St Mary Westout and St Peter annexed, abutting north to the highway through the town to Winterbourne, south to the field of Thomas Sherman called Hozescroft'*.[9] Horsecroft Field is now the site of Spring Cottage, Camoys and Rotten Row

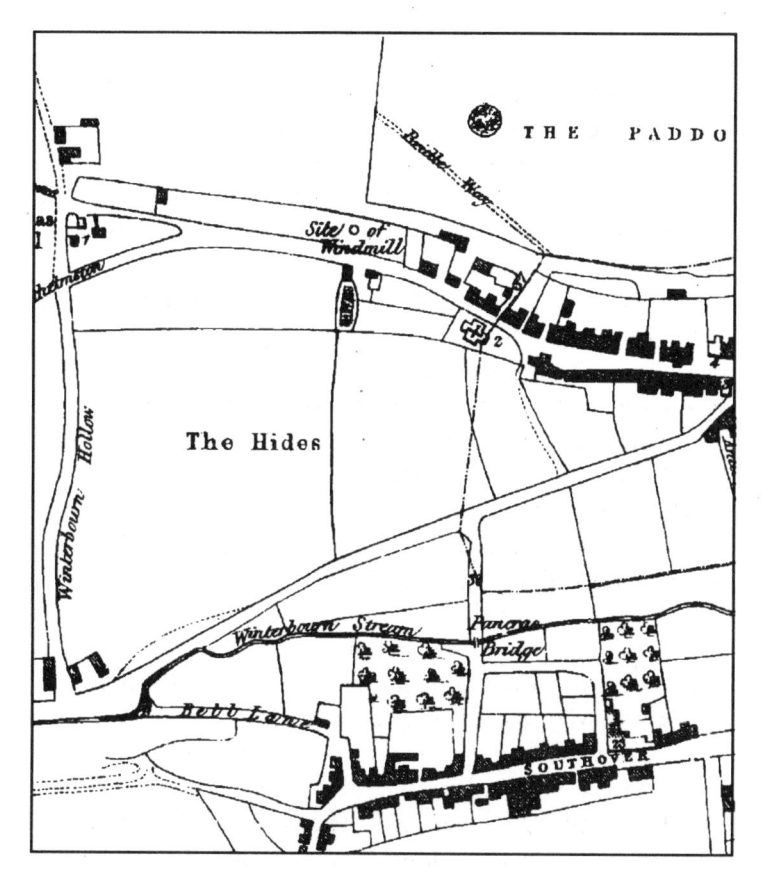

Figure 7.2. Westout, based on William Figg's map, c.1775.

House, and for the property to lie between Horsecroft and the road to Winterbourne it must be placed on the southern side of the road. Rykehurst, Pikehurst and Kykehurst all appear as alternatives to the name of the original donor, but the deeds of St Anne's charities give 'Parkhurst'.[10]

An early building on the site of St Anne's House at No. 111 was owned by William Storer in c.1570, and by Thomas Storer in 1624. This was the most significant property held of the borough manor, which had land up the hill as far as No.

114, and down to Rotten Row. The Storers also tenanted another croft to the west which ran up as far as No. 118, and possibly No. 117. This was held by William Spence in 1676 of his eighth part of Houndean Manor.[11] The houses with intervening numbers appear in different ownerships at later stages, due to development by Storer and his successors. The street numbers are also confused (e.g. Nos. 116-7 were once numbered 112-3). Nos. 112-4 had once been part of Thomas Storers' croft, and by 1691 were four small houses, becoming three in 1717, of which the central property was owned by Jacob Tonson (or James Johnson). Tonson was a close friend of Thomas Pelham-Holles, Duke of Newcastle, and they were both members of the Kit-Cat Club. He was said to be a frequent visitor to Newcastle's Claremont.

At the western limit, before St Anne's Church Lane, the house called 'The Croft' (with 'Allington' and 'Westoute') occupies St Peter's Church Croft, also held of Houndean, referred to in 1639 as the Parsonage Croft.[12] This had on its street frontage the site of the manor pound. In 1401 John Springaunt was granted land here fifty feet by two feet *'by the Lord's poundefolde'*.[13] Development had begun in the sixteenth century, and modern Nos. 121-3 had become 'the Church House' by around 1570. The pound itself was moved to Abinger Place in St John sub Castro in 1800.[14]

Church Lane (the name of the lane having been taken recently from All Saints Church Lane, which has been downgraded to Church Twitten) probably represents the boundary between St Peter's and St Mary's church crofts, and perhaps earlier of the parishes, for it and land to the west (now the County Hall car park) was St Mary's croft, again Houndean manor land. The dividing line is still marked outside the drive entrance to the Croft by a square with the letter 'E' (for John Every).

Across the High Street there was a piece of land, part of which seems to include the eastern side of the Pelham Arms, called the Slipp or Wellfield.[15] This presents a problem, for there is another 'Slipp or Well Croft' on the opposite side of the road beyond the western end of St Anne's Church, and the names seem not only to be used indiscriminately, but are both occasionally referred to as the 'Wellfield'. Some sixty feet wide from east to west, it then provided, as it does now, a way out of the High Street northwards, past a well which gives rise to the modem name of Well House Place, and then crosses the Paddock. This was called the 'Wellhouse' in 1790.[16] It was listed as having twenty occupiers, and these may represent the 1796 comment by Paul Dunvan *'... on the fourth day of september 1794 was laid the first stone of Mr John Button's academy, in a small field of this parish called the Well Croft. The plan of this building is not less judicious than the prospect from it is rich and extensive. Indeed for excellence of site, accommodation and system of instruction, it is justly considered one of the best infant seminaries in Great Britain'*.[17] This sounds like an advertising puff, for John Button abandoned the site and moved his academy to Cliffe shortly afterwards.

Down the hill was a property held by the borough called 'The Hermitage' in around 1570.[18] There is no known explanation for this name, but in a period when people did not call their properties by romantic names, it could be an endowment given to and let on behalf of the Anchoress in St Mary Westout Church. However, this does leave a substantial, unaccounted-for gap between the recorded house name of 1570 and the Anchoress, who seems not to have lasted much beyond 1300. It would have been quite a small property in the area of Nos. 130 or 131.

At the western edge of Nos. 134-5 there was a passage *'to north lane'* (now Paddock Lane) which was still a public pathway as late as 1824, and for which evidence may yet remain.[19] Between 1624-1683 the quit-rent for this property grew from sixpence to seven and a half pence, reflecting the 'bridging over' of the passage by No. 135 some time after 1624.

Although there have been gaps in its continuity as an inn, Shelley's Hotel has a claim to be among the oldest pubs in Lewes, appearing first in 1526 when, in the Court of Star Chamber, John and Joan Mason successfully dispossessed two individuals of ownership.[20] The 'Chantry House' of Sherman's Chantry is now considered to have become the site of the Old 'Free' School, but this may not be the case. In 1806 a bundle of deeds entitled 'Chantry House' described it as land *'belonging to a part of the garden and ground of the mansion house of Henry Shelley Esq in St Ann's Lewes being that part which lies between the mansion house and the free school'.*[21] This may imply that the eastern end of Shelley's car park was part of the original holding.

The chantry was a type of chapel built separately on its own site, established by a wealthy person or body, whose endowment supported the perpetual saying of mass for the founding family. In 1450, Thomas Brasyer sold lands called the Hyde to Thomas Baker, who was in the process of changing his name to Sherman. John Sherman, his son, held land from the manor of Hide when he wrote his will in 1474, and died then or shortly afterwards.[22] He had 'lately' built a chantry chapel in St Peter's churchyard in Westout and endowed it with a rood of land (a quarter of an acre) and a tenement and garden (the Chantry House), and lands in Chiltington, Kingston and Arlington, the revenues from which were to support the chantry and its priest.[23] The site of the chantry chapel itself is now somewhere beneath Nos. 108-9 High Street.

John Sherman's brother Thomas increased the endowment in 1498.[24] It produced a total income of £10 12s 8d, to which were added obits from other parts of the town and from various other persons, bringing the annual income to £22 7s 1d. Against this, various payments had to be made, leaving £10 17s 0d for the poor of St Michael's, All Saints, St Peter's and in the town at large. One obit provided for eight shillings to be paid yearly to the poor of St Peter's *'in the churchyard of the said church'*, presumably by or near the chapel itself. Christopher Dugdall was the chantry priest at the time of its suppression in 1547. He drew £8 8s 11d from the revenues. In 1545 *'... the said Preiste ... surrendred up the said chantry ... upon a pension agreed between them'*.[25] It possessed a chalice weighing ten ounces and valued at £1 16s 8d. The assets of the chantry were granted to Henry Tanner and Thomas Bocher of London on 28 March 1549,[26] and were bought from them by John Kyme.[27]

Kyme left the chapel and two houses to his sister Joan, then to his sister Elizabeth and then to Seth Aucocke, who in fact inherited.[28] Kyme sold the *'Chapel lands'* of sixteen acres in East Chiltington to Richard and William Wood in 1558-9[29] and left to his sister Joan Kyme *'the chapell landes' in Arlington and Willington'* [sic], with lands in Houndean, Ashcombe, Smithwick (being then in Kingston) Barcombe and Plumpton. The Chantry House itself was later owned by Mrs Mary Jenkins of Chelsea, and she let it to trustees for use as a dwelling house for the master of the Free School, along with provisions for education and for augmentation of the staff salaries. The old premises in Southover were given up when the school moved here in 1714, but once each year it was the custom for the pupils and master to make a pilgrimage back to Southover. The High Street site was a fine, timber-framed building of four gables, as can be seen in an illustration of 1830 (Figure 7.3), before it was replaced by the present, equally fine building. Approaching the old Westgate, No. 141 (142 as originally numbered) was the 'Kings Head' in 1683, but it is also referred to as *'The Kings Head sometime the Black Boy'*.[30] By 1851 it had become the St Anne's Workhouse.[31]

John Rowe, whose work has been a great help to so many historians of Lewes, appears surprisingly infrequently in the records himself. Apart from bits of land which appear in his temporary custody in his role as steward for Lord Abergavenny, he seems to have avoided owning a house in the

Figure 7.3. The Free School on St Anne's Hill around 1780.

town, preferring to rent from others. St Wilfrid's at No. 143 High Street (144 originally) has been identified as his, but it was not quite as simple as that, because this street number covers a collection of copyhold properties, and in 1622 the site was held by his brother Thomas Rowe. Thomas held *'two tenements and a barn, two stables three gardens and two orchards ... a tenement in which John Rowe Sr. lives ... another tenement ... and a garden'*.[32] By 1624 all this had passed to John Rowe Jr., Thomas's son and John's nephew. So all one can be sure of is that John Rowe Sr. did live here, in part of his brother's property, at the end of his life.

Both Mark Anthony Lower and William Figg claimed that a Mr Newdigate was living in Lewes in 1745, and could be identified with the Sir Roger Newdigate who gave the Newdigate Prize for poetry at Oxford. Walter Godfrey, however, described this as *'most improbable'*.[33] The evidence is that Susan, the widow of Stephen French, owned this property in 1683.[34] She married Thomas Newdigate of Lewes in 1696 as her second husband. They had children, Charity,

Richard and John. Charity Newdigate died unmarried and John, as youngest son, inherited the copyholds in 1721.[35] In 1747-8, a Sir Roger Newdigate of Arbury in Warwickshire, heir of Roger Newdigate of Lewes then deceased, sold the property. The weak link in this chain is that it is not established that Roger Newdigate was any relation to Richard and John, but surely the unusual name, the coincidence and the fact that we have a Sir Roger Newdigate inheriting and selling this property, should at least give Lower and Figgs' statement some credibility.

At this point we can consider the Pest House, the Poor House and the Hospital of St Nicholas, known as 'the Spittle', which spread over into St Mary's parish. Although they were separate buildings, their history is inter-linked in a complicated pattern. The tangle of conflicting sources is such that most workers who have attempted to sort them out give up and go away. For those wishing to know more about the legal application of the Poor Law in Lewes between 1750-1840, Ann Baker's monograph on this subject is to be commended.

The Pest House was bought in 1742 when a group of forward-thinking citizens decided to institute a safe house for the confinement of persons suffering from smallpox, but also any other *'infectious distemper'*.[36]

Residents who lived in the borough, Castle precinct or any house between the Spittle and the borough boundary could have use of it. A house was obtained in a field to the west of St Anne's church, already referred to above as the Wellfield, later called the Pest House field. In 1769 this forethought paid off, when a public meeting summoned by the constables agreed to appoint a watch for the Pest House, while Henry Blackman, his children and his wife, who had the smallpox, were there, together with John Ade and his family. It seems that the idea was that any family at risk should go and live there, supporting themselves. There seems to have been no question of medical or financial support.

In 1775 the Fellowship resolved to pay three shillings per

week to Richard Stacey who kept the house well-aired when there were no patients there. The 1806 Town Books consist purely of pages of recitation of deeds, since all the trustees had died and no one had been appointed to replace them. The last known trustee was John Reid ('Haberdasher of Hats') who died in 1786.[37] He left his property to his son-in-law Richard Hatchman in right of his wife Ann, and owing to the failure to appoint new trustees, ownership of the Pest House passed to Reade's only daughter, Hatchman's wife. Ann Hatchman was pressured into selling the property to the Fellowship for a peppercorn. New trustees appointed themselves.

By 1804 the Pest House had already been reported as being *'in a useless and dangerous state ... being near the highway and other houses'*, and by 1806 the constables, having recovered control, called a public meeting to decide whether it could be sold off. By this time there was insufficient demand following the advances made by vaccination against the disease, particularly after 1794. It had for some time previously been leased to the churchwardens of St Anne's parish as the parish poor house, enabling them to sell their previous poor house. Horsfield writing in 1824 says that *'when the utility of the Pest House had ceased it was converted into a Poor House for the parish'*.[38]

When the borough sold the Pest House, they did so, *'for the most money that can be gotten for the same'* to the officers of the parish of St Peter and St Mary Westout, and the £450 proceeds was lent to the commissioners for paving the borough, at interest. The officers of the parish raised the purchase price in 1808 by a loan for 1,000 years.[39] The site is now that of the water reservoir beside the turning from Western Road into County Hall.

In St Peter's parish the Poor House had been at the site of Nos. 121-3 High Street. The property backed on to St Peter's Church Croft. It first appears around 1570 as *'The Church House'* of the parish, and by 1624 was owned by the rector, but occupied by John Eager. In 1753 it is first described as the *'parish workhouse and garden'*.[40] In 1808 it was held by Joseph Goldsmith (a carpenter), the parish overseer of the poor, who was also a churchwarden. It then took the form of two houses in the front, and two in the rear, reached by a central passage, which in 1812 Goldsmith sold for the parish to Josias Smith. Smith demolished the rear pair of houses in 1831.[41]

Dunvan now introduces a note of confusion into the record.[42] He suggests that a poor house belonging to the parish of St Anne's, and the croft adjoining it, were the site and part of the endowment of the Hospital of St Nicholas Westout. What he seems to be saying is that when the Poor House was built on the street frontage of St Anne's Hill it was built as an adjunct to the hospital. This would have been in the fifteenth century or earlier. St Peter's Church Croft was part of the endowment of the Hospital of St Nicholas.

The Hospital of St Nicholas straddled the whole triangle of land at the junction of Nevill Road, Brighton Road and Spittle Lane. It is said to have been founded by the Priory around 1085, for thirteen poor brothers and sisters, but (unlike St James' Hospital in Southover) it does not appear in the Priory chartulary, and it is more likely that it was founded by William de Warenne. The endowment consisted of six cottages, a garden and a small croft. This is something of another muddle. The site is clearly visible in Figure 7.4. There is a map by John Deward dated 1618 on which the Spital Houses are shown to be four in a terrace row.[43] Dunvan relates how there were so many hopeful candidates that they were queuing up outside waiting for corpses to be removed, but then says that through the good management of the overseers of the poor, it had by his time become *'a scene of morality'*, as well as providing humane accomodation.[44] In view of its subsequent history this is not easy to accept. Horsfield has an illustration, but otherwise deals with hospitals in general rather than this one in particular.

The earliest documentary record shows that the hospital

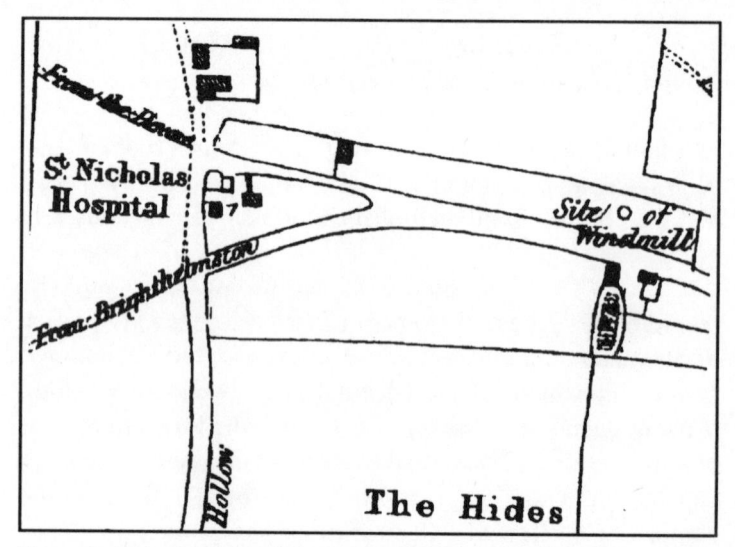

Figure 7.4. The Hospital of St Nicholas Westout, based on William Figg's map, c.1775.

was held in 1624 by William Inyans of the borough, paying a quit-rent of twelve pence. It then disappears from view until 1809, when Thomas Partington, counsel, recorded that the churchwardens of St Anne's, despite the fact that they had no deeds, claimed immemorial use of the hospital as a poor house for the parish.[45] He thought it doubtful that anything would give them good title to the property, but a month later the churchwardens and overseers claimed to hold the property in trust for the parish.[46]

They agreed to convey the western part, and any title they could claim to the rest, including a small property belonging to Moses Henty on the northern side. Clearly trouble was brewing, for in 1818 Courthope related that:

> *Soon after the erection of Lewes Barracks on Mr Verrall's land opposite the Spital, Thomas and William Kenward erected a bakehouse and tenement on adjacent land held of Houndean manor to supply the soldiers and their families and also fifteen or sixteen*

single room huts which were let to soldiers for the purposes of co-habiting with their wives, the huts encroached four feet onto a parish road. The sale ... in 1809 was prompted by its unsuitability as a poor house in view of the proximity of the barracks. Since the demolition of the barracks the huts have been let to 'persons of the lowest, most debauched and worst description, property in the neighbourhood being deemed unsafe and the morals of the younger part of society debauched to an extent almost beyond description, in fact a nest of beggars, thieves and whores.[47]

Strong words, even for the period. Since the Kenwards proposed to do nothing about the conditions, Courthope suggested that they be indicted for encroachment on to the highway, with the costs to be paid from the rates. This seems to have brought the Kenwards round, and after some haggling over the price, they sold it in 1819 to the inhabitants of the parish for £500, the money being put up by prominent citizens.[48] Part of the property was sold in 1864 and the remainder in 1901, and the proceeds invested.[49] In view of the history of the site trustees were appointed by the Charity Commission according to a scheme of 24 April 1868. There is said to be a rent charge of 18s 4d in aid of the Spittle on land and hereditaments in the High Street of Westout, property of the Marquis of Abergavenny. This appears in the outgoings from Sherman's Chantry. There is an enigmatic entry in Rowe (p.54) where the Reeve of Worth parish in the manor of Ditchling was excused 13s.4d of payments due, *'for the Spittle of Lewes',* which may represent some commutation of tithes.

This is not easy to sum up, but on the dissolution of the Priory, no-one seems to have known whether the Spital was Priory property or not, and with the usual laissez-faire attitude of the citizens, it just carried on regardless, with St Anne's churchwardens and overseers doing what they could to keep it under control. Parts of the site were excavated in 1994 by the Field Archaeology Unit, and an interim report mentions the discovery of over 100 burials.[50] Over a period of some 700 years, a property housing thirteen poor, old and sick people would easily have produced 100 burials, but the interim report mentions internments from the Battle of Lewes, and also identifies five corpses with head wounds, bound hands, and in one case with an ankle manacle.

St Mary Westout

St Mary Westout is an entirely different parish, and consisted mainly of agricultural land outside the borough. It is a muddle of different and shifting manorial ownerships, and it serves little purpose to sort them all out. However, some study does help to identify the early manorial ownership of areas now built on, such as St Anne's Crescent, Baron's Down, Houndean Rise and Winterborne Close. From St Anne's church westward to the western end of the parish near Housedean Farm, lands on either side of the Brighton Road were in different manors. On the southern side, these were Winterbourne, Smithwick and Breadnore. To the north their equivalents were Spittle, Houndean and Ashcombe. Only Spittle and Winterbourne had land on both sides of Winterbourne Hollow, and it will be easier to deal with the lands on the eastern side first before crossing the hollow and venturing west.

Neville Road separates the Spittle area lands into eastern and western parts. The western Spittle lands are now the Prison, Southdown Avenue and Houndean Crescent, all of which were absorbed later by Houndean Manor. Spittle Farm and Croft at the junction of Spital Road and Neville Road are all that was left east of Neville Road after the western part had been absorbed into Houndean. They were sold in 1603-4, bounded to the south by the Lewes to Brighton Road, and to the east and north by the Lewes to Ditchling Road. They were by then not truly a manor, being held in private ownership. In

1755 John Earl de la Warr leased barn and lands called Spittle Farm. He sold it to Richard Trevor, Bishop of Durham. Finally, in 1800, Viscount Hampden (the Bishop of Durham's heir) sold a barn and lands, part of Spittle Farm in St Peter and St Mary Westout and St John sub Castro, Lewes, to John Tourle of Landport and St John sub Castro.[51]

Winterbourne Hollow divides the Winterbourne Manor lands to west and east. The locality was known as Winterbourne in AD 966, when it was the property of St Peter's Cathedral in Winchester, or rather the Abbey of Hyde, a dependancy of St Peter's.[52]

Winterbourne's southern limit fell where the bridge now goes over to Winterboume Close, and beyond the bridge was Southover Manor land called the 'Pewits' (an earlier spelling being the 'Puets'), for which I have not been able to find an explanation. By Domesday, Winterbourne was held for one hide. Division between east and west took place and the western part became absorbed into Houndean. What remained east of the road adopted the alternative name of Hyde. In 1450 Thomas Brasyer conveyed to Thomas Baker, alias Sherman, lands called the Hyde.This implies that the lands were already separate from the manor, which continued as a separate entity called Winterbourne. In 1595-6 Edward, Lord Abergavenny, rented out what looks like this part only to William Lane, for three 'lives'.[53] Later the old 'Manor House' was leased, described as *'That old messuage or tenement called Winterbourne and a little parcel of land adjoining and lying open to the Hides, containing about 30 acres, and bounded by Winterbourne Hollow on the west, to Rotten Row on the south, to the parsonage croft and the churchyard on the east, and to the land of William Lane and Richard Knight'*, (which although it does not say so, must be to the north).[54] The thirty acres defines the whole, but bits passed in and out of different ownerships.

Hide in Westout was described as a manor and croft in 1630.[55] There were perhaps a few odd scraps of land elsewhere (Sherman's Chantry House in St Peter's is an example) which justified the description of 'manor', but effectively it was a collection of pieces in private ownership from which all manorial rights had been removed. Dunvan makes the confusion worse by writing that the manor of Winterbourne is the same as the manor of Hyde, which had changed its name to the manor of Westout, and in any case belonged to the Priory of St Pancras, held jointly with the manor of Southover. This arises from a description of it in 1608 as the manor of *'Hide Maries Westout'*.[56] These comments are nearly correct, but before they can be accepted at face value we need to identify what happened before that. By 1525-6 Thomas Sherman had bought the land on which St Anne's Crescent was later built, and in 1573-4 he with his son and heir (another Thomas) sold all of this to William Lane of Southover. The bounds were the Hides to the south, the road from Offham to Southover to the west, the lane from Lewes to Brighton to the north, and the croft and windmill of J. Inkershall to the east.

At this point the Victoria County History states that *'nothing further is heard of this Manor'*, but in 1712 William Lane of Southover (and his wife) sold the manor of Hyde. At this time it was bounded to the north by land held by William Pellatt (the St Anne's Crescent land as above), and to the east by the parsonage and churchyard. Thus by then there were two separate parts, one continuing the name of the Hides, and the other an unnamed but vestigial remnant of Winterbourne Manor. These were sold in 1713 when Lane sold Hyde to Nathaniel Trayton, and although I have not found documentary evidence to support it, it appears to have been left by Trayton to Durrant, together with Southover. Trayton was not particularly interested in the niceties of manorial rights, only in capital value or rents, so Winterbourne and Hyde effectively disappear into Southover, which he already owned. Thomas Horsfields laconic comment *'Recently this manor has passed in the same line of possession as the manor of*

Southover', is therefore correct.[57]

Moving now to the west of Winterbourne Hollow, the boundary between Winterbourne and land called Smithwick was the lane that now leads to Hope in the Valley and continues down to the Winterbourne stream. The western limit of Smithwick was the Ashcombe Hollow, now the busy link between Kingston and the Brighton Road. Much effort has been expended in the past in attempting to establish a non-manorial identity for the 'manor' of Smithwick, which was probably not a manor at all. It does not appear in Domesday. The earliest reference is 1147 when St Peter's, with the chapel of Smithwick, paid a half mark (6s 8d) to the Priory.[58] The chapel belonged to St Peter's, and this presents a problem, since the site of Smithwick Chapel was in the middle of the parish of St Mary. It must be assumed that St Mary Westout is a later creation which included a large area once in St Peter's parish, where the chapel remained. The chapel and the alleged manor of Smithwick seem to have disappeared by 1487.[59]

The division beyond Ashcombe Hollow is at the 'Green Bank', still marked by a railway bridge over what is otherwise a private farm road from Ashcombe Farm towards Kingston Hill. This was Breadnore, and was once part of Kingston Manor. It extends as far as Littledown, but it became part of Ashcombe Manor and lost its separate identity.

On the northern side of the Brighton Road, there were similar dividing lines at Houndean Bottom leading to Houndean Barn. This parts Spittle on the east from Houndean to the west. Houndean was separated from Ashcombe by an extension of the lane serving Ashcombe Farm. The manor of Ashcombe held two hides in Domesday. It had an unspectacular history, having been held with the manor of Poynings until the reversion was bought by Thomas Sackville, Lord Buckhurst.[60] Over the years bits of Ashcombe were 'captured' by Houndean. There was, for example, until at least 1825, a field on the eastern side of the entrance to Ashcombe House and Farm, called *'Chaple* [sic] *field',* but it has not been possible to tie this in with the chapel of Smithwick.[61]

Houndean Manor is the real trouble-maker in this area. On the death of Edmund Lenthall (1484) it was divided into two, one part of which passed to George, Lord Abergavenny. The remainder was divided so that by 1608-9 Thomas Sackville, Duke of Dorset owned a quarter of the whole, the remaining quarter being, after several shifts of ownership, held by 1737 by John Spence of Malling. In 1831 the Sackville quarter had been obtained by the Earl of Abergavenny. To make matters more confusing, in 1615 the Sackvilles took a lease (for three lives) of much of the Abergavenny Houndean lands, so where they owned a quarter of the manor, they also held another half by lease. This can lead to the land ownership being misunderstood, and identified as freehold when it was leasehold, or vice versa.

I have tried to separate out the history of the various areas in St Mary Westout, but the shifts in land or manorial ownership are perhaps only important to the specialist. The land is there, the ownerships are varying and inconstant. Railways and the Lewes bypass now occupy much of the area.

Chapter Eight
The Suburb of Southover

There has been so much history written about the great Priory of St Pancras that the rest of the suburb of Southover has not had the attention it deserves. Just where Southover fitted into Lewes at Domesday, and what it was part of before the Conquest, is still in dispute. Rowe considered it to be part of the borough of Lewes.[1] The borough of Southover claimed in 1552-3 *'... of old antiquity and custom out of time beyond the memory of man, to nominate one of two parliamentary burgesses from Lewes to each alternative Parliament'*, and so saw itself as separate from the neighbouring town.[2] It is difficult to be sure that it ever exercised this power, however, and, in any case, it later fell into disuse.

Dunvan suggested that Southover was an alternative name for Niworde, the pre-Domesday manor from which Lewes was carved out.[3] On this basis he claimed that as the earliest reference to the name of Southover is in the Priory chartularies before Domesday, the whole manor of Niworde passed into the possession of the Priory.[4] So he applies to Southover *'every circumstance recorded of Niworde in Domesday'*. This cannot be accurate, since it implies that up to the death of Edith, widow of Edward the Confessor in 1074, William de Warenne had been making grants out of the land before he is recorded as having taken possession. He and Gundred were in Cluny in 1076. The Priory was not founded until one year later, in 1077, and its continued existence remained in some doubt until 1087, when the charter of foundation was confirmed. The surviving charter, although considered to be a forgery, is more probably a reconstruction of a genuine document, although one has to treat it with some reservations. It established that at least part of the Southover peninsula was within the land owned by the de Warennes. *'I ...*

have given ... the land also which is called the Island beside the monastery with meadows and grazing lands. Also all the land which I had in demesne within the island on which the monastery is situated ...' [5] This implies that land on the island was held in two ways, requiring two separate mentions, one being in his demesne, one in some other tenure.

Southover was not a hundred.[6] It was described as a halimote in 1249 and 1263. In 1275 it was said to be a half-hundred but, if this were so, it fails to provide an answer to where or what the other half was. A halimote or halmote, is a normal manor, with courts baron and leet. Southover does not appear in a 1439-40 list of the hundreds.[7] In 1540 and 1560 Southover was described as a hundred, as it was again in 1587,[8] but this description referred specifically to individuals registering for a lay subsidy, and it does not appear in any wider or later context.

The parish of Southover was a thirteenth-century creation, and there is little that can be added to the accounts of it in the Victoria County History, supplemented by my guide to the church and parish. The southern boundary of the parish has moved backwards and forwards due to the pressure exerted by the Priory and the resistance put up by the parishes of Iford and Kingston. It has included at times both the Upper and Lower 'Rises', but there was here always a battle with Iford parish, which Iford seems to have won, over both. To the west, the boundary is the parish of Kingston, a twelfth-century creation, and to the north a strangely straight line suggestive of a surveying, runs in common with St Anne's as far as the bottom of Keere Street. Thereafter it follows the old borough boundary to Watergate Lane, where both drop down to the Winterbourne stream, and then along the stream to the Ouse, where the line parts company with the borough boundary by turning south along the river.

There had been a wayside chapel on the peninsula from an early, pre-Conquest period, and this could have been among the first churches in the area. It was the subject of the earliest foundation charter, and formed the nucleus of the later Priory. The charter describes it as '... *a church which we had converted from wood into stone ... which had been from old time dedicated to St Pancras ...*'[9]

When Lewes expanded beyond its western walls and a new borough boundary was drawn just short of St Mary's church, the land so included, although part of the borough of Lewes in every other sense, remained firmly within Swanborough Hundred. It is likely that Southover was as exclusive, but the records are not available. If ownership by the Priory and the pressure it exerted resulted in the creation of something called the Hundred of Southover, then by 1831 the land had reverted back to Swanborough Hundred.

Perhaps none of this matters too much. Southover was in any case a separate entity. Between 1074 and 1086, after the Conquest, William de Warenne began the series of land grants that created the Priory and led to the administrative arrangements that defined Southover. What we see from later information is that land in the parish may have been divided into separate, 'sacred and profane' holdings. The Priory and its' lands, situated mainly on the eastern side of the peninsula, was held by knight's service, which obliged the holder to provide military assistance to the crown in times of need. This explains why Prior John de Charlieu (in office from around 1364-96), while leading in person the defence of the region, was captured during a French raid. The land outside the Priory precinct, the 'profane' holding lying mainly at the western end, was held by 'in socage' tenure. This included not only the land in Southover, but also the extensive Southover holdings in Lewes. These did not carry the military obligation, and could be sold or inherited without restriction.[10] The de Warennes specified in this kind of grant to the Priory that '... *lands shall be free and quit of all things and customs...in the borough*' and '...*discharged and quit of all secular services and demands* ...'[11] Where such properties were gifts made by individuals, and there are matching deeds in the Priory chartulary, some land could still be subject to annual quit-rent payable to the de Warrenes. In 1568 Edward Boocher of Mayfield, who may have been acting as an agent for the crown, sold property to Anne Pelham and her son Thomas, much of which was once under the control of the Priory.[12] In many of the conveyances of this series, John Stempe held the lay manor of the borough of Southover. Stempe must have sold large parts of its holdings, whether in Southover or Lewes, by creating freeholds, or very long leaseholds, which lost their original manorial identity. Much of the Lewes property given to the Priory was transferred in such substantial blocks that any underlying pattern is obscured. However, a distinction can be seen where the Priory lets property subject to payment to the lords of the borough of Lewes on the one hand, and to the Priory on the other.

There is no conflict between the Priory owning its own precinct, and owning land in the borough by another form of tenure. Ownership by these distinct means was continued by Thomas Cromwell, who leased much of the Priory precinct to Nicholas Jenney for twenty-one years in 1539-40, while retaining the borough himself. Both manors continued in Cromwell's ownership until his death in 1541. The crown then conveyed both elements separately to Anne of Cleves, but confirmed Jenney's lease, which still had some twenty years left to run. The borough manor was sold separately to John and Anne Stempe after Anne of Cleve's death in 1557.[13]

Thomas Sackville, Lord Buckhurst, with Sir Richard Baker (his father-in-law), bought the Priory manor in 1559, at the end of Jenney's lease. Then what remained of the borough manor, after the Stempes had sold much of it, was bought by Sackville in 1582, from whom the title descended through the female line until, in 1710, Richard Tufton, Earl of Thanet sold it to Nathaniel Trayton.[14] The Trayton ownership continued until Thomas Trayton conveyed to his son Nathaniel all of the manor lands, except those of Rev. Edward Newton. This consisted mainly of Southover Grange and three acres of Ades

Brook, the East Ham, Carters Wish and the Priory lands. This may be further confirmation that the Priory lands remained separate from the lay manor, as did the Grange lands, which by then seem to have been sold out of the manor. The Priory Manor continued in existence, but gradually lost its separate identity after the abolition of the distinction between tenure in socage and tenure in knight's service in 1660. Ownership can be seen to continue through the Durrant family, successors to the Traytons, who in 1836 sold land from the Priory Manor, including the site of Priory Crescent, then part of *'Upper Lord's Place'*, for development.[15] In the conveyance, Upper Lord's Place carried with it an obligation to pay £17 4s 8d to Sackville College, *'among and together with others of great value'*. Meanwhile the borough manor ran in parallel, based at the site of the present manor house opposite Anne of Cleves House. It passed from the Durrants after about 1835 into the possession of William Verrall, and continued through the Southover branch of the family to Frank Verrall by 1940. William Verrall was a brewer of Southover and seemingly part of a separate branch of the main Verrall family in Lewes. His father was John Verrall who died in 1708, and it was his son William who bought the manor and all its rights. He died in 1890 aged 92.[16]

Nicholas Jenney's lease is a confused pattern of old religious and later lay descriptions. After reserving the church, cloister and the *'House called the Frater'*, so that any uncompleted work of destruction could be continued, it grants *'... all houses, buildings gardens crofts, meadows and marshes within the precinct of the Priory wall ...'*, amounting to roughly twenty acres. This limits the precinct to the present Priory grounds, bounded to the east by the wall which runs southwards from the Mount, to the west by Cockshut Lane, and to the south by the line of the Cockshut stream. In a reply to an enquiry he had received in 1772, the Rev. Robert Austin, incumbent of St Anne's, stated that the old walls of the Priory were still recognisable, and although the wall on the southern side seemed modern, traces of the original turf-covered ridge could be found.[17] He showed that on this basis the whole area of the precinct occupied thirty-nine acres, two roods and nineteen perches. Measuring from modern maps the total area amounts to 38.68 acres, from which deducting 17.67 acres to the east of the Mount leaves 21.02 acres.

On the western side of the Priory church, forming the western range of the cloister, were the Prior's lodgings, approximately where the barn and the extension to the church burial ground are now. Cluniac priories were laid out to a very consistent design, so the layout of the Prior's lodgings is likely to have followed that at Cluny, and can be seen in detail at the better surviving example at Castle Acre Priory in Norfolk (Figure 8.5).[18] The lodgings were listed in the lease as the *'Hall Place'*, the *'Pantry'*, *'Wynesellers'*, the *'Chequer'*, and the *'Old Store-house'*, and there was a new storehouse with a counting house over it. These were all grouped near the western door of the church. There was also a gallery, which is difficult to place, but if the Castle Acre plan is an accurate guide, then it would have been situated on an upper storey. Also in this area must have been the chapel. As the church, cloister and frater were in the centre of the site, they divided it into western, southern and eastern parts. The lease, like many similar documents, really requires a plan or map, as the descriptions are confusing.

Access to and from the *'new buildings'* of the Priory kitchen and bakehouse was through the *'Great Malthouse'*, which was the second and larger reredorter re-named. The new buildings were in the eastern third of the site, the kitchen and bakehouse being known to have been in the western third. The new buildings were above and below (i.e. at one end or the other) of the great chamber, which seems to have been what is now called the infirmary hall. The great chamber is separated from the *'Upper Chamber'* by an *'entry'*, and this may be the cross-passage at the western end of the hall, between the hall and the dorter. These descriptions of *'chambers'* are post-Dissolution substitutes for whatever their original names had been.

Outside the grounds there was a garden adjoining the new buildings and the great malthouse. This must have been where the present memorial to the Battle of Lewes stands, as another garden and orchard lay between the malthouse and the *'millpounde'*. Millpounde refers to the dam or bank impounding the mill water, which in the lease was bounded at the opposite end of the malthouse by the gardener's house. Excavations in 1969-70 revealed something of the water-control system, whereby a pounded area of water could be released, when needed, to flush the reredorter drains. This is the origin of the name Cockshut, and has nothing to do with the characteristics of the flight of the woodcock. There was a pounded area of water called the Pool, now overlain by the railway, which stretched back into the marshy land to the west of Cockshut Lane.

Jenney also held half of the great pigeon house, the proctor's barn and stable, the *'Fysshe house'* and the *'Pond Garden'*, and had free fishery in the mill pond and the *'Podpole'*. The earlier names of *'Podpole'* and *'Lortepole'* must all refer to the Pool. In 1618 William Aucocke held a watermill within the Priory wall, and this was presumably close to the millpound, inside the Cockshut Lane boundary wall of the precinct.[19]

So Jenney leased all of the Priory precinct, except for a chunk taken out of the middle, and it included the Prior's lodging. His lease expired around 1560, and almost immediately Sir Richard Sackville and Sir Richard Baker (his father-in-law) appear as owners of the land, of which they may well have bought the reversion. Sir Richard Baker's share came to Richard Sackville via his wife. The borough element of Southover was still owned at the time by John Stempe. In 1582 Sackville bought the borough from Stempe and thus reunited the two areas and the two different tenures.

Following this brief review of land ownerships in

Southover, we can now look at some of the principal early buildings which survive in the suburb. Much has been written in the past about Southover Grange, some of it misleading. In what follows, I have used the name of Sackville to provide a common thread, rather than introduce his alternative titles of Buckhurst or Dorset, except where these have a specific bearing on events. William Newton, described in some sources as a builder, was born in Cheshire in around 1516, and came to Southover in 1549, to live at what is described by a later successor as *'the Priory of St Pancras'*. Godfrey thought that Newton could have bought the Grange in 1549, when he came to live there, and says that it had previously been the property of Agnes Morley (quoting her will). There is however no record of the Grange in the interval between the 1512 probate of Agnes Morley's will and a 1548 chantry certificate, nor any evidence of a conveyance.[20] The only early reference to Southover Grange dates to 1535, where it appears as '*Le Graunge*'.[21]

The grange, if it was part of the Priory in 1549, could only have been bought from Anne of Cleves, as Nicholas Jenney was still tenant of the Priory precinct, including the prior's lodging, at that time. If Newton was there at all, then it could only have been as Jenney's sub-tenant. Ten years later Jenney was constable of Southover, in the year in which his lease came to an end. Sackville and Baker bought the area corresponding to Jenney's lease in that year. Whatever Newton bought in 1549 may well have included the Grange, but it could not have included the *'Lord's Place'*, as the Prior's lodging came to be known after the Dissolution. Horsfield claimed that the first William Newton was steward to the Sackvilles, but from other sources it can be shown that Richard Amherst was the steward at this time.[22] The error may have originated in a reply sent by the Rev. Robert Austin in 1772, in which he refers to *'William Newton, one of (the present) Mr Newton's ancestors, Steward to the Earls of Darset, died in 1648, aged 84'.*[23] The Sackvilles did not

THE SUBURB OF SOUTHOVER

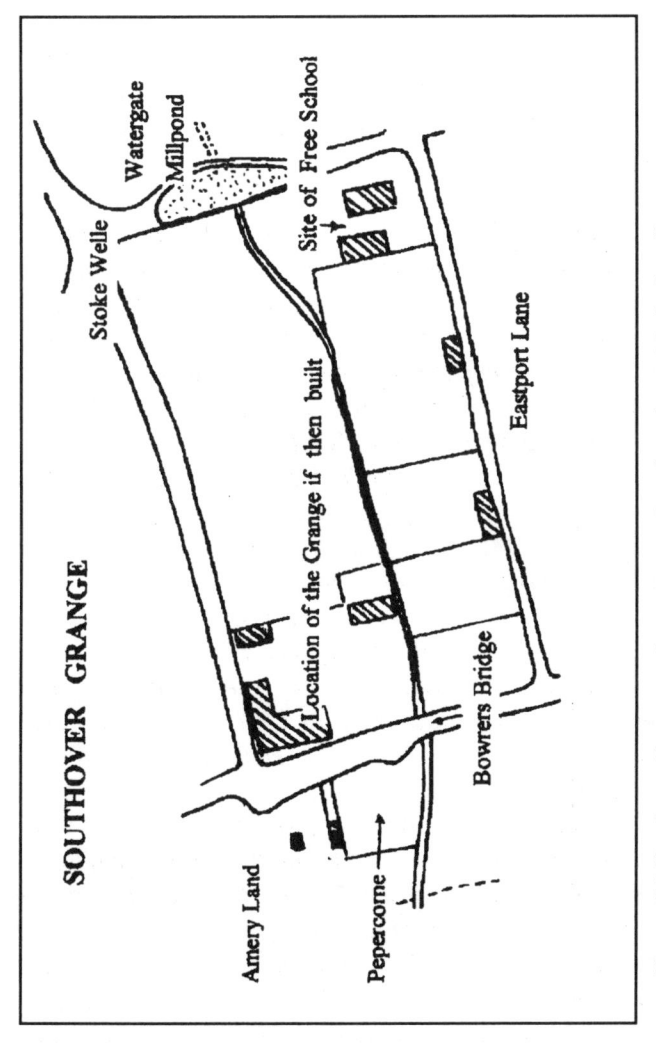

Figure 8.1. Southover Grange and its environs. Based on Agnes Morley's will c. 1511-12, and recent Ordnance Survey maps.

become Dukes of Dorset until 1604, so if this statement is taken literally, then the steward mentioned must have been the second William Newton, b.1554.

The date of the Grange, constructed by the first William Newton, is generally believed to be 1572, based on a date upon an original fireplace within the building. The guide notes to the house state, quite correctly, only that this date *'has usually been taken as the year of the erection'*. The story of the ruin of The Lord's Place, destroyed by fire in 1568, is based on a letter from Sackville in which he states that *'A hous of mine in the country by sodein chaunce of fire was burned'*.[24] Sackville owned Buckhurst, as well as Lewes Priory, in Sussex, and Godfrey has suggested that it was Buckhurst which burnt down. Sackville drew up substantial rebuilding plans for this property at the time, even though these were not carried out. Sackville signed deeds in 1596 *'at his house called the Priory of Lewes'*.[25] This again suggests that the Prior's lodging was still habitable at that date. The first Earl of Dorset died in 1608. Austen says that Mr Newton showed him a portrait of the last earl to have resided at the Priory, *'in whose time the accident happened'*. He adds a marginal note referring to that William Newton, *'Supposing him to have been fifty four when he built, the fire must have happened before the year 1618'*. This seems to fit the facts better. In 1662, the Earl of Thanet (who had succeeded to the Sackville lands) is shown in the hearth tax retuns to be holding a property with thirty-three hearths in Southover. John Farrant, in the introduction to the volume, claims that *'... the Earl of Thanet evaded liability for 33 hearths at Southover Grange'*, and quotes from his source, describing *'an ruinous and useless house for the most part fallen downe and lying waste'*.[26] I fear he may be wrong as identifying this as the Grange, as the tax records state that Apsley Newton was then living there and was assessed for eleven hearths. What Thanet owned must have been the remains of The Lord's Place, ruinous by then perhaps. In 1965, N. E. S. Norris claimed that *'Southover House, the*

Lewes mansion of the Sackvilles, was formerly the Prior's lodging of Lewes Priory ... an excavation in 1955 traced some remains of this building below a market garden...according to excavation evidence, there had been a fire c.1600-1625.[27] However, the phrase *'some remains ... below a market garden'* implies that the excavation was not at Southover Grange, but presumably in the market gardens which still form part of the Priory site.

The Lord's Place, whether burnt or not, remained in Sackville ownership throughout the period, and seems to have become derlict around 1618-25. The Grange may once have been part of the Southover Borough holdings, and may have been bought by Newton from Stempe after 1557. Agnes Morley's will is lengthy and repetitive, but contains information which I believe has not been considered before. *'Item, I will that Thomas Puggislee the Elder ... shall have all my landes and tenementes, sette and being in the parrishe of Southovere aforesaide, between the course of the water ryning frome Bowrers Brigge unto Watergate uppon the southe, the Kinges high waye ledying frome the said Bowres brigge toward Lewes on the west, and the kynges high waye ledying under the towne walle of Lewes thurgh Stoke Welle towards the mylle at the Watergate upon the est and northe ...'*[28] This describes the lands of Southover Grange, but the only tenements mentioned in the will are those occupied by the Free School and the master's and ushers house, which were south of the Winterbourne stream in the south eastern corner. The will goes on *'... I will that Roger Puggislee shall have my messuage and a garden thereto belongyng called the Pepir Corne ... Betwixt the Kinges high waye leading from Bowrers briygge towards Lewes upon the east. And the lands and tenements of the Aumours [*i.e. almoners*] of the Pruiory of Lewes on the west, southe and northe'.*'This seems to establish that her house was on the land west of Southover High Street opposite the Grange, now the car park of the primary schools, and not the Grange itself.

Figure 8.2. St John, Southover, by Lambert.

So it seems unlikely that Southover Grange existed in 1512. It was built at an unknown date, but 1572, the date on the fireplace, is as good a guess as any. The grange continued in the Newton's ownership until the last century, and in 1808 Colonel Newton bought the site of the Old Free School at the corner of Eastport Lane and Gardener Street (as it was then), to add to the lands of the grange.

Another building which has caused some controversy is Southover church (Figure 8.2). Randoll's Map of 1620 has thumbnail sketches of All Saints, St Michael's and St John sub Castro which reasonably represent those churches as we know them from other records, while St John's, Southover, appears so entirely different from the one we know that, uncomfortable though it may be, the shape he shows has to be seriously considered. To the east are the remains of the great gate of the priory, and this corresponds with later information and illustrations. Other sources show that there was a house between the church and the great gate (now taken up by the nineteenth-century chancel extension).[29] The tower of St Michael's, Lewes, shown with a long tapering spire on Randoll's Map, looks much as it does now, and is at the western end of the church. So perhaps the tower that fell down at St John's, Southover in 1698 was the fourth round tower of the Ouse valley. It was possibly when rebuilding began in 1711 that the tower was moved to the western end.

There is no evidence for a south aisle in Randoll's Map. It has been suggested that the southern arcade represents the divisions between the male and female sleeping areas in the building, which was originally the hospitium of the priory. However, the present south wall is considered to date to the post-Dissolution period, with windows taken from the priory and reset there. This, and the absence of a south aisle on Randoll's Map, must raise a query over its suggested medieval date. To create a south aisle requires the piercing of an arcade through what was previously the southern, outer wall of the church. The present arcade, although contrived with plain

UNKNOWN LEWES

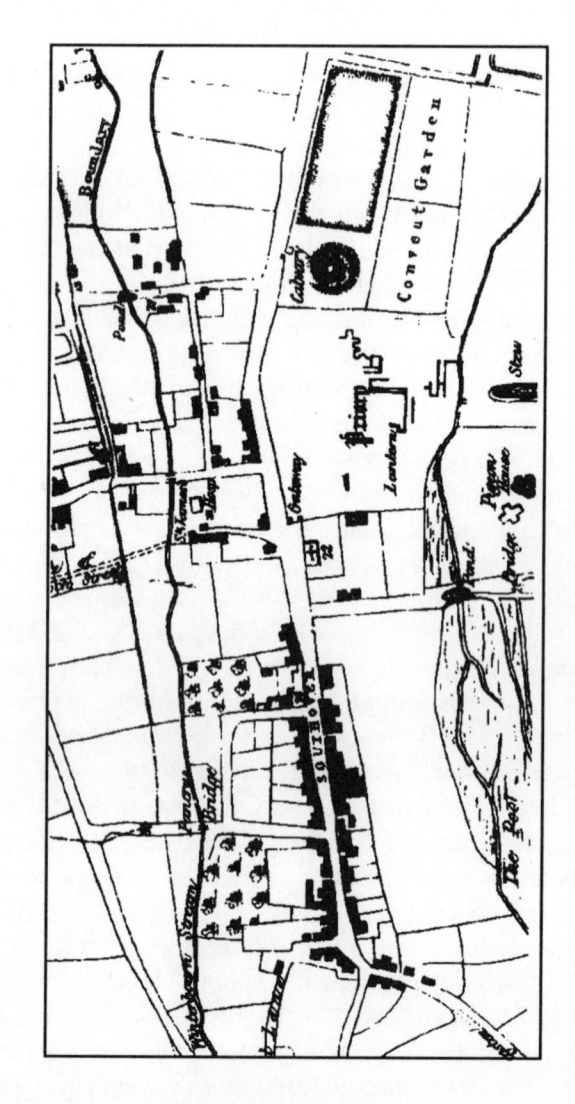

Figure 83. Detail of Southover from Figg's Map of c. 1775.

semicircular arches, and looking authentically Norman and no later than the late twelfth century, has no mouldings, and the arches are plastered so that the details of the masonry are obscured. They could equally well have been re-used from the Priory. They also spring from quite unnecessarily massive drum piers, large in diameter and short in height. Drum piers similar to these can be found in some of the great Norman cathedrals. For comparison, the much smaller drum piers in St Anne's can be studied. They could have been re-used curved arches originally supporting the lavatory cubicles in the great reredorter of the Priory, and would fit the dimensions. The arrangement remains at Castle Acre, Norfolk, where curved arches of this type remain in situ. The Priory was a source of stone for many houses in Southover, and of ready-masoned curved stones, whether for arches or drum piers. The westernmost pier is partly engaged with the later west wall, and we know that the whole of that wall was rebuilt during the building of the new bell tower. All one can reasonably claim is that the south aisle was built between 1560 and 1714.

Anne of Cleves House is an important property in Southover High Street, and while it may have belonged to the manor in her time, it was freehold by 1910. It is not recognisable in the manor roll of 1618, although messuages of Edward Lyndsey, Anthony Stapley, Paul Garwaye (called Saunders), and tenements of Edward Brooke (two), John Knoll, Anthony Stapley, Lancelot Lennard (?Kennard) and Thomas Kirke do appear.[30] If it can be identified with one of these, then it was then part of the manor, but it is more likely to have been sold off privately by the Stempes. It was bought by the Verrall family at auction and given to the Sussex Archaeological Society, at that time being let to three-weekly tenants. Verrall also gave the north-western range, now containing the Wealden iron and Lewes displays, and once a malthouse, to the Society in 1928. It may be proper to put on record here that the staircase to the upper levels of the west wing is an addition of 1937. The fifty spockets, eight uprights

UNKNOWN LEWES

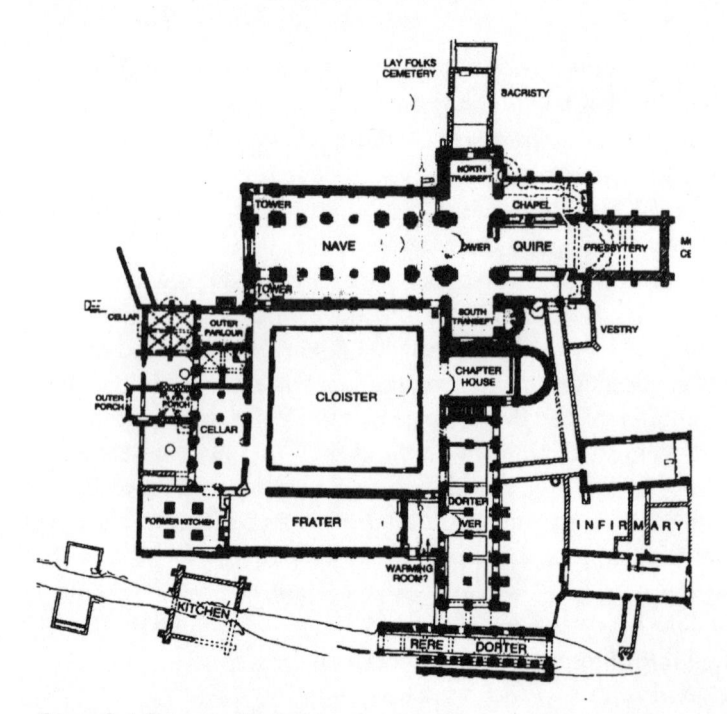

Figure 8.4. Priory at Castle Acre.

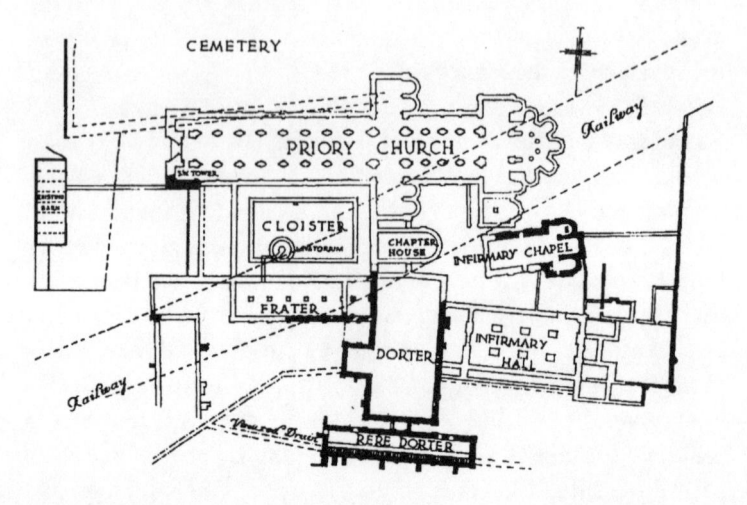

Figure 8.5. Priory of St Pancras, Lewes.

and twelve braces in the 'bedroom' (which are part of the rather strange roof-framing there) were installed in 1928, and the vertical post in the 'Oak Room' supporting the cross junction of the ceiling is an insertion of 1933.[31]

Chapter Nine
Conclusion

So there we are, with all the defects and contradictions that this sort of work is prone to. Looking back on what I have written, and the thirty years I have lived in Lewes, I believe I should conclude by trying to put down what has made the experience so worthwhile. If you go up Mill Lane, Malling, at the end of the tarmac surface you will find a pathway on the right hand side. This leads uphill to the old Romanised route which connected the Caburn block of Downland with the Lewes-London road. As it winds up over the flank of Malling Down a view of Lewes gradually opens up, and when you reach the open down at the first dew-pond, it is worth sitting down to take it all in.

The view from the Castle is, of course, more dramatic, but it gives one the feeling (as any castle should do) of dominating the town and its surroundings. From Malling Down, however, one can see all one wants to, without any one feature of the town becoming over-dominant. The most noticeable thing visible in the panorama spread out below is the large area of modern Lewes which I have not mentioned at all. This is the area of Malling and Cliffe, and I have left them out because I have been mainly concerned with Lewes up to about 1850, before which Cliffe, Malling and Southover were all separate local government entities not involved in or with the history of the town. I have looked briefly at Southover only to introduce some alternative viewpoints to the established history. The merger of the three suburbs with Lewes in 1881 to form a single local government unit makes sense when you see them from up here, but the desire for local identities means that these new areas still keep themselves separately identifiable within the town. The river is, of course, a natural barrier between Cliffe, Malling, and the town, as is

CONCLUSION

the Winterbourne stream the dividing line between Lewes and Southover. These boundaries are important, and need to be respected. The grey artificiality of local government can impose an amorphousness on what should be a living community

Immediately below is the area of Malling Brooks, now filling up with industry, warehousing and supermarkets. This expansion was necessary, and Lewes was fortunate in having a lung of land of this size on its own doorstep. The 'historical' industries of the town and suburbs would have in any case needed space to grow, and there would not have been room for them to do so inside the older industrial areas. Indigenous industry, such as Russell and Bromley, and Avery the weigh-scale manufacturers, are examples of locally-born industries which had to move elsewhere. Baxters, the printers, with a long history behind them in the town back to the eighteenth century, have expanded on their own site, but this must surely now have limitations. On the other side of the river at the foot of the hill, the thread of commerce cloaks either side of School Hill, with tourism, the professions and local government preponding. Then the town climbs up to the Castle, and then on beyond to the modern County Hall.

So, if one looks back to King Alfred and the earliest days of the town, one can still see something of his philosophy. Defence, the immediate and primary reason for the town, has now a lesser or non-existent role, except perhaps in the hearts of the people. If the need for castles, militia and local regiments has gone, law and order still have an important part to play. To the right, the bulk of the Sussex Police Headquarters above Malling is clearly visible. That the Sussex police force should have its base in Lewes is no more than a continuation of the Alfredian pattern. Up on the hill, the bulk of the old County Hall, now the Crown Courts, still shows its presence in the town, and down at a lower level, the new Magistrates Courts in Friars Walk reinforce it. Administration is perhaps the best represented of all the Alfredian functions, since the headquarters of the County and District Councils are in the town, and the Town Council (having the more limited functions of a parish council, but with some fund-raising capability) inhabits offices in the Town Hall. It is the quality and application of the Town Council that will decide whether Lewes can be maintained as it is. However critical one may be, the Town Council members are local and they know something of local ways and needs. The District Council has two disadvantages, first that the members from the area outside the town will always outnumber and outweigh the local members, thus spreading and evening out the total view, but also because for the council officers to gain promotion it is usually necessary for them to move elsewhere. Thus, before any officer, and particularly a planning officer, can get to know and understand the forces that lie behind the history of the town, he leaves and another is appointed in his place.

The market is still strongly present. There are those who lament its changing nature and cry 'empty shops in Lewes!', but if a market is to have vitality then there must be room for change, a seed bed in which to nourish one of the basic functions of the town. The early mint, of course, no longer survives, but its successor, the joint-stock banks and building societies, still have a strong presence in Lewes, and in the case of one at least, have in the town a regional head office with a specifically commercial emphasis.

In an increasingly lay society, religion and the church are still represented, while not as strongly active as they once were. Lewes proper may be over-furnished with Anglican churches (and the Church of England faces grave problems in deciding what pattern will overcome this problem) but it still has its suffragan bishop, its archdeacon and its rural dean. Beyond that, the Roman Catholics have an undeniable presence which would have been unthinkable 150 years ago. It is sad that Methodism no longer flourishes, although Unitarianism still has a strong presence. United Reformed, and Baptist Churches, and the Society of Friends, continue the

CONCLUSION

principle of dissent which has always been a feature of Lewes's religious life. So, even if the churches of Lewes present a rather diverse appearance at first sight, nevertheless the Council of Churches maintains progress towards a more unified approach.

Credit must be given to two bodies, the civic society, and the chamber of commerce. The civic society, known as the 'Friends of Lewes' has by no means been supported by everybody in the town, not out of indifference (the usual fate of such bodies) but out of strong disagreement with some of its policies. It can be said, however, that the activities of the society have contributed much to a town which has maintained its integrity, its small scale, its intimacy, its friendliness, and finally, but by no means least, its beauty. There are many buildings which have gone, some of which have been replaced by less than worthy successors. Some attempts have been made to introduce modern 'toothpaste' architecture, mainly by the big national retail chains, but not only has this been successfully resisted, but one example where the ground floor of adjacent properties began to spread outwards, was thwarted. It has been with some considerable effort that this restraint has been exercised.

Equally, the policies of the chamber of commerce have had a similar effect. Many years ago the chamber decided that the day-to-day commerce of the town must gravitate to the bottom end of the High Street, to link up with the Cliffe shopping area, and that tourism and the 'up-market' shops should be at the top of the hill, with the professionals and local government in the middle. It has worked consistently to achieve this, even though it has no better tool to use than enthusiasm and encouragement, and it has been a long haul over years to achieve it.

So, if you will sit with me on Malling Hill and look down on the town, you will see that most of the elements that King Alfred decided should be there, are still there. You will also see a town rejoicing in its own personal integrity, uninfluenced by the much bigger towns which flank it. You know when you are in it, and when you are out of it. It has a hard edge. In some ways, that hard edge may represent the quality of the king's special peace, the distinction between town and country. Lewesians do not forget, as they look out on all sides to the surrounding country, that they have a foot in both. This was an important factor eleven hundred years ago, and to preserve this feeling is to preserve the town. The defence of the town is now carried out in a much wider theatre, but Lewesians would not be backward in responding to any call should the need arise. Despite much local carping, the new County Hall buildings in St Anne's do not dominate the Castle. All the elements of local government administration, at government, county, district and town levels, can be seen from Malling Hill. You can see the new County Highways Authority office building, the fire station and headquarters (a far cry from the days of the giant hooks for pulling off burning thatch), and the headquarters of the ambulance service. If you peer round the corner you can see the domestic refuse tip, successor to the days of amercement for casting out stinking fishwater. In fact, if you know where to look in the first place, you can see almost anything you wish, and can take your mind back to the times when records, or even intelligent interpretation of the times before records, reach back into the distant past. Beyond the horizon and beyond the king's special peace towards Falmer is the University of Sussex. While Lewes had its schools, of many and various kinds, the University is an influence which for better or worse will dominate the future growth and life of the town. The influx of faculty members has had a significant effect, adding a column of academic influence where previously defence, administration, law and order, market and mint, and church sustained the town. It is most welcome, provided it is there as an additional element, and does not pull down any of those elements which have upheld the town so stoutly in the past.

    I made a few inadequate acknowledgements in the

CONCLUSION

introduction to those who have helped me find sources and understand the forces that have moved history. My wife has barely read a word, and so in that sense has had no influence at all, but I could not have managed without her continued support of my work, or without her encouragement over low periods, or her suggestions of how to get around obstacles, and of her desperate attempts to get me to write intelligible English. It is therefore to her that I owe my real thanks for making this book possible.

John Houghton
Swanborough, Lewes
Autumn 1997

Notes

Introduction
1. W. G. Hoskins, *The Making of the English Landscape*, Hodder & Stoughton, 1992, p. 219.

Chapter 1.
1. *The Hundred and the Hundred Rolls*, Merlin Press, 1930.
2. H. P. Finberg, *The Formation of England 550-1042*, Hart Davis, p. 121. 1930.
3. F. W.Maitland, *Domesday Book and Beyond*, Fontana.
4. Maitland. Op. cit.
5. Maitland. Op. cit.
6. Maitland. Op. cit.
7. Morris (editor), *Domesday Book (Sussex)*, Phillimore, 1976, pp. 25d, 26a.
8. Public Records Office Cat. Inq. PM 1.711 53 HenIII 1268-9.
9. *Sussex Record Society*, Vol. 40.
10. East Sussex Record Office LAN294.
11. *Sussex Archaeological Collections*, Vol. 114, p. 179.
12. G. N. Garmondsway (translator), *Laud Chronicle (E)*, Dent, 1953.
13. Birch (editor), *Cartularium Saxonicum*.
14. C. E. Blunt, *Coinage of Athelstan*, BNJ, Vol. 42, p. 7.
15. *Sussex Archaeological Collections*, Vol. 118, pp. 322-3.
16. See also *Sussex Notes & Queries*, Vol. 6, p. 83.
17. *Sussex Record Society*, Vol. 38, p. 4 and *Sussex Notes & Queries 6*, p. 83.
18. Richard Coates, *Some place names of the Downland Fringe*, Younsmere Press, 1990, pp. 12-21.
19. Coates. Op. cit.
20. *Anglo-saxon England*, Clarendon, 1971, p. 265, note 2.
21. D. Hill, The Burghal Hidage, *Mediaeval Archaeology 13*, 1969, pp. 84-92.
22. Morris (editor), *Domesday Book (Sussex)*, Phillimore, 1976.
23. Meaney, *Gazetteer of Anglo-saxon burial sites*, Allen & Unwin, 1964.
24. Birch (editor), *Cartularium Saxonicum*.
25. *Sussex Record Society*, Vol. 38, p. 1 and p. 50.

NOTES

Chapter 2
1. Whitelock (translator), *The Anglo-Saxon Chronicle*.
2. D. Hill, 'The Origins of the Saxon Towns' in *The South Saxons*, pp. 187-9.
3. *Sussex Archaeological Society Newsletter*, March 1975.
4. *Sussex Archaeological Collections*, Vol. 114, p. 194.
5. East Sussex Record Office ADA 165 (Copyholds, St Johns parish, p. 36).
6. East Sussex Record Office DYK 1123.
7. East Sussex Record Office Aber 1 fo 82.
8. Horsfield, *History of Lewes*, Vol.1, p. 165.
9. Dunvan, Op. cit.
10. East Sussex Record Office ADA 156. fo2.
11. *Sussex Record Society*, Vol. 34, p. 9.
12. *Sussex Archaeological Collections*, Vol. 113, p. 76.
13. *Sussex Archaeological Collections*, Vol. 114.
14. *Sussex Record Society*, Vol. 69, p. 127.
15. *Sussex Record Society*, Vol. 34, p. 69.
16. Public Record Office SC6 HenVII 1474 quoted in *Sussex Notes & Queries*, Vol. 5, No. 3.
17. *Sussex Record Society*, Vol. 34.
18. Jeremy Haslam, *Early medieval towns in Britain*, Shire Archaeology, 1985, p. 42.
19. *Sussex Archaeological Collections*, Vol. 89, pp. 133-4.
20. *Sussex Archaeological Collections*, Vol. 124, p. 125.
21. *Sussex Express*.
22. British Library, Add.Ch C30627.
23. *Sussex Record Society*, Vol. 40, pp. 4, 6 etc.
24. *Sussex Archaeological Collections*, Vol. 124, 1986. 'Burgage Tenure & Topography in Lewes', pp. 119-28.
25. *Medieval Southampton*, C.Platt.
26. *Sussex Record Society*, Vol. 34, p. 16. I am grateful to Mr.Whittick for the translation.
27. M. de W. Hemmeon, *Burgage tenure in medieval England*, Cambridge, Mass., 1914, p. 77.
28. Searle, *Lordship and Community 1066-1538*, Pontifical Institute, Canada, 1974.
29. East Sussex Record Office SAS Map E5.
30. *Transactions of the Lewes Scientific & Literary Society*, Vol. 1 No 3, p. 68.

31. Public Record Office, SP Dom Case A No. 6.
32. *Sussex Record Society*, Vol. 38, p. 91.
33. M. de W. Hemmeon, Op. cit., p. 104.
34. Public Record Office SC6 1474. Incidentally, this continues '... *extending in length from the high street which leads from Bretale towards the barres of St John which is on the west and the lane stretching from the High Road leading from Fisshestrete and which leads from Bretaxle aforesaid towards Greenewall on the east over against the croft late of William Oviotte and the croft of John Trankmere and a croft of William Cheeseman on the east and west from the land land late of John Parker on the north and east as it is known of old by meets and bounds ...'* This is a good example of a deed guaranteed to make a researcher go cross-eyed.
35. Ibid.
36. East Sussex Records Office SAS A223.
37. Public Record Office, SC6 6158 DL29 7312.454.
38. East Sussex Records Office Aber1 Fo.24v.
39. Pers. comm. Mr. C. Whittick.
40. Cal Anc Deeds A4217. 1383-4.
41. Cal Anc Deeds A 4089.
42. Cal Anc Deeds A4091/4138.
43. *Sussex Record Society*, Vol. 40, p. 2 & Cal.Anc.Deeds A.4199.
44. Cal Anc Deeds A4186, 4190 and 4091.
45. 1378 Poll. AMS 3056.
46. A15551 1308-9.
47. *Sussex Record Society*, Vol. 40, p. 3.
48. Public Record Office, SC6 6158 (1532-4).

Chapter 3

1. This theory was first put forward by A.H.Allcroft in Sussex Archaeological Collections, Vol. 63 and 64, and led to much acrimony between him and L. F. Salzmann.
2. *Sussex Record Society*, Vol. 38 p. 35.
3. Pipe Roll 25 HenIII.
4. *Sussex Archaeological Collections*, Vol. 113, p. 76.
5. Beamish, *Battle Royal*, Fred'k Muller Ltd, 1965.
6. e.g. Beamish, Op. cit.
7. David Carpenter, *The Battles of Lewes and Evesham*, Mercia Publications.
8. Carpenter. Op. cit., p.26.

NOTES

9. Allcroft, *Downland Pathways*.
10. Beamish, Op. cit.
11. Horsfield, *History of Lewes*, Vol. 1, p. 255.
12. W. H. Godfrey, *The Priory of St Pancras*, 1927, p. 12.
13. *Victoria County History of Sussex*, Vol. 7, p.16.
14. Ibid., p.21.
15. *Sussex Archaeological Collections*, Vol. 91, 1953.
16. W. H. Godfrey, *Lewes Castle*, various editions of guide book.
17. *Sussex Record Society*, Vol. 34, pp. 185-91.
18. G. M.Trevelyan, *Illustrated English Social History*, Vol. 2, p. 170.
19. *Sussex Record Society*, Vol. 48.
20. Ibid., p.44.
21. Ibid., pp 74 & 77.
22. Personal observation.
23. *Sussex Notes & Queries*, Vol. 15.
24. Woolgar Mss. Vol 2. Barbican House Library.
25. East Sussex Record Office Aber1 fo.42.
26. LBGS Handbook in possession of the writer.
27. Copy of letter in Sussex Archaeological Society Business archive, made by this writer.
28. SAT 97.
29. SAT Letter book H59.
30. *Records of the South Saxon Lodge*, G.Grantham, 1964.

Chapter 4

1. Morris (editor), *Domesday Book*, Sussex, Phillimore 1976, notes after 'land of Richard son of Gilbert', & *Sussex Archaeological Collections*, Vol. 102, p. 68.
2. *Sussex Record Society*, Vol. 40, pp. 7 & 23.
3. Cal Anc Deeds 4114.
4. British Library Add Ch 30569.
5. *Sussex Record Society*, Vol. 44.
6. Ibid.
7. Walter Map, c.1181, quoted by Helen Cam in *The Hundred and the Hundred Rolls*, p. 59.
8. *Victoria County History of Sussex*, Vol. 7, p. 20 quoting Ass.R.921 m.13d.
9. 1750 East Sussex Records Office ADA 159.
10. East Sussex Records Office A4133.

11. *Sussex Record Society*, Vol. 48.
12. East Sussex Record Office DYK 1123.
13. East Sussex Record Office SAS PN1.134.
14. *Sussex Record Society*, Vol. 69.
15. C. R. V. Bell, *A History of East Sussex County Council 1889-1974*, Phillimore & Co. Ltd, 1975, pp. 8-9.
16. *Victoria County History of Sussex*, Vol. 7, p. 20.
17. British Library Add.Ch 30556.
18. Public Record Office DL 7312454.
19. East Sussex Record Office SAS EG253.
20. *Sussex Record Society*, Vol. 38, p. 25.
21. *Sussex Record Society*, Vol. 40, p. 25.
22. *Sussex Record Society*, Vol. 34, p. 120.
23. *Sussex Archaeological Collections*, Vol. 11, p. 225.
24. East Sussex Record Office Will A5/144 (will 1558 probate 1563).
25. East Sussex Record Office ADA 45.
26. Public Record Office SC6 Hen VII 1474.
27. *Sussex Record Society*, Vol. 48, p. 2.
28. Ibid., p. 16.
29. *Sussex Notes & Queries*, Vol. 15, p. 3.
30. *Sussex Record Society*, Vol. 48, p. 40.
31. *Sussex Record Society*, Vol. 34, p. 124.
32. *Sussex Record Society*, Vol. 48, p. 34.
33. Ibid., p. 91.
34. Dunvan, p. 345.
35. Notice of sale.
36. Essays of a traveller, 1750.
37. John West, *Town Records*, Phillimore & Co., p. 103. The whole chapter 'Gild and Borough ordinances c. 1066-1600' is of great value in understanding this matter.
38. East Sussex Record Office Dyke Hutton Mss 11.22.
39. Ibid.
40. East Sussex Record Office ADA 156, 6.7 & 8 Ja 1, East Sussex Record Office AMS 30560, 30603.
41. *Sussex Record Society*, Vol. 48, p. 74.
42. *Sussex Record Society*, Vol. 54, p. 193.
43. *Sussex Record Society*, Vol. 34, p. 120.
44. *Sussex Record Society*, Vol. 48, p. 104
45. Ibid., p. 24

NOTES

46. Ibid., pp. 58-9.
47. *Sussex Record Society,* Vol. 69, pp. 129.
48. *Sussex Record Society,* Vol. 48, pp. 32-5.
49. Ibid., p. 61.
50. G. Holman, *Some Lewes Men of Note,* Baxter, 1905.
51. *Sussex Record Society,* Vol. 34, p. 16.
52. *Sussex Record Society,* Vol. 48, p. 20.
53. Ibid., p. 111.
54. Ibid., p. 22.
55. *Sussex Record Society,* Vol. 698, p. 192.
56. *Sussex Record Society,* Vol. 70, p. 291.
57. Sussex Record Society, Vol. 48, p. 111.
58. Ibid., p. 102.
59. *Sussex Record Society,* Vol. 69, p. 28.
60. Ibid., pp. 71-2.
61. *Sussex Record Society,* Vol. 69, p. 119.
62. East Sussex Record Office, BLE C2/1 1-3.
63. Sussex Archaeological Society, Notes & Queries, Vol. XV No. 1.
64. Ibid., p. 133.
65. *Sussex Record Society,* Vol. 69.
66. 16 Geo.III.

Chapter 5

1. *Sussex Archaeological Collections,* Vol. 68, p. 176 quoting PRO Anc. Deeds A14181.
2. *Sussex Archaeological Collections,* Vol. 93, p. 29.
3. Marchant, Map of Lewes and Southover, 1824.
4. *Sussex Notes and Queries,* Vol. 12, p. 86, 160, 175.
5. *Sussex Record Society,* Vol. 38 and 40.
6. *Sussex Notes and Queries,* Vol. 9, No 2.
7. Add.Mss 30575.
8. Dunvan. p. 350.
9. B.Lib Add.Mss A 4185.
10. B.Lib Add Mss 39339/87.
11. Victoria County History, Vol. 7, p. 38.
12. *Sussex Notes and Queries,* Vol. 9, No. 6.
13. *Sussex Archaeological Collections,* Vol. 45, p. 40.
14. Personal communication. Mrs.F.Anderson.

15. *Sussex Record Society*, Vol. 11, p. 378.
16. B. Lib., Add.Mss 30572.
17. *Sussex Express & County Herald*, 20.11.1877.
18. East Sussex Record Office SAS WH 180.
19. *Sussex Archaeological Collections*, Vol. 38, p. 200.
20. *Sussex Archaeological Collections*, Vol. 13, p. 24.
21. *Sussex Archaeological Collections*, Vol. 45, p. 40.
22. Domesday Book 10.44, and 10.63.
23. *Sussex Notes and Queries*, Vol. 2, p. 252.
24. *Sussex Archaeological Collections*, Vol. 45, p. 40.
25. *Sussex Record Society*, Vol. 46, Bo 60.
26. *Sussex Record Society*, Vol. 40, p.6.
27. *Sussex Archaeological Collections*, Vol. 68, p. 266.
28. *Sussex Record Society*, Vol. 40, p. 23.
29. Public Record Office, SP Dom Case A No 6.
30. Public Record Office, SC6 MA 474.
31. Sussex Archaeological Society, Library open shelves.
32. L&P Hen VIII 13(1)g.384.74.
33. *Sussex Archaeological Collections*, Vol. 68, p.172.
34. Chich.Episc.MSS Lib A f 5r.
35. *Sussex Record Society*, Vol. 46, p. 60.
36. East Sussex Records Office SAS HC 592.
37. For Southover, see East Sussex Records Office A2229/2.fo.11, for Ringmer see East Sussex Records Office SAS E518
38. East Sussex Record Office SAS E/5.
39. B. Lib., Add Ch 30553
40. *Sussex Record Society*, Vol. 40, p. 22.
41. *Sussex Record Society*, Vol. 11, p. 9.
42. J. Houghton. Personal examination.
43. *Sussex Record Society*, Vol. 34.
44. BL Add Mss 30564.
45. *Sussex Record Society*, Vol. 40, p. 4.
46. *Victoria County History*, Vol. 2.
47. Personal communication. Mrs. F. Anderson.
48. *Sussex Archaeological Collections*, Vol. 134, pp. 71-123.
49. Poland, op. cit., p.87.
50. *Sussex Record Society*, Vol. 38, p. 5.
51. G. Mantell, Gideon, *A Day's Ramble in Lewes*, 1846.
52. *Victoria County History*, Vol. 7, p. 21.

NOTES

53. G. Mantell, *A Day's Ramble in Lewes*, 1846.
54. L&P Hen VIII xiii (2) 1060.
55. L&P Hen VIII xix (1) 9182(52).
56. East Sussex Record Office SAS Map E/5.
57. Woolgar. Mss. Spicilegia. Barbican House library.
58. 1784. James Lambert, in Burrell collections at B.Mus.

Chapter 6

1. 31 Geo.3.
2. Maitland, *Domesday Book and Beyond*, Collins, Chapter 9, 'The Boroughs', pp. 235-7.
3. Frank Barlow, *Edward the Confessor*, Eyre & Spottiswoode, London.
4. View of Frankpledge, 1617.
5. *Sussex Record Society*, Vol. 38, pp. 7-9.
6. *Sussex Notes and Queries*, Vol. 4, p.116.
7. N. P. Blaker, *Sussex in byegone days*, 1919.
8. Blaker, op. cit.
9. *Sussex Notes and Queries*, Vol. XVII, No. 2, p. 49.
10. Carl Bridenbaugh, *Vexed and troubled Englishmen, 1590-1642*, Clarendon, Oxford, 1968.
11. Rothwell (editor), *English Historical Documents III 1189-1327*, Eyre and Spottiswoode, 1975.
12. *Sussex Record Society*, Vol. 40, pp. 2 and 6.
13. *Sussex Record Society*, Vol. 54, p. 193.
14. *Sussex Notes and Queries*, Vol. XV, No 1.
15. *Sussex Record Society*, Vol. 48.
16. Ibid. p. 72.
17. Elliott's Mss. Eastbourne Public Library.
18. I am grateful to Mr. Mike Helps who obtained copies for me of the building contract.
19. 31 George III.
20. *Sussex Archaeological Collections*, Vol. 107, 'The Lewes Market', p. 87 et. seq.
21. G. P. Elphick, *Sussex Bells and Belfries*, Phillimore, 1970.
22. Thomas Dicker's daughter Emily Winter Dicker married the Rev H. M. Lee, and their youngest son was Arthur Lee, later Viscount Lee of Fareham who (using his wife's money) gave Chequers to the nation as a home for the Prime Minister.

Chapter 7

1. East Sussex Record Office SAS Aber 1.
2. Horsfield, *History of Lewes*, Vol. 1, p. 264.
3. Woolgar, *Spicilegia*, Vol. 1. Barbican House Library.
4. *Sussex Notes and Queries*, Vol. 8, p. 216 (c.1870).
5. *Sussex Record Society*, Vol. 34, p. 235.
6. *Sussex Record Society*, Vol. 43, pp. 98-9 and *Sussex Notes and Queries*, Vol. 13.
7. Kent Archive Office U269 E184.
8. *Sussex Record Society*, Vol. 36, p.142.
9. East Sussex Record Office C/8/2/1.
10. East Sussex Record Office AMS 5809.10.
11. *Victoria County History*, Vol. 7, p. 35.
12. East Sussex Record Office AMS 5745.3.
13. Public Record Office SC6 MA 1474.
14. *Sussex Record Society*, Vol. 69, year 1800.
15. East Sussex Record Office SAS A 506.
16. Woolgar, op.cit., Vol.1.
17. Dunvan, op.cit., p. 373.
18. Kent Archive Office U269 E184.
19. Marchant, Map of Lewes,1824.
20. *Sussex Record Society*, Vol. 16.
21. East Sussex Record Office AMS 3007-3080.
22. *Sussex Record Society*, Vol. 43, pp. 88-9.
23. *Sussex Record Society*, Vol. 36, p. 27.
24. *Sussex Notes and Queries*, Vol. 13, p.318.
25. *Sussex Record Society*, Vol. 36, p. 111.
26. Pat 3 EdwVI Part v.im cal vol ii p.421-2 quoted in *Sussex Record Society*, Vol. 36, p. 111.
27. Ibid.
28. *Sussex Archaeological Collections*, Vol. 100, pp. 133-4.
29. Ibid., p. 115.
30. East Sussex Record Office SAS WG 200 and FA 83-4.
31. East Sussex Record Office 1851 Census.
32. East Sussex Record Office ADA 156.fo.17.
33. Sussex Archaeological Collections, Vol. 93.
34. East Sussex Record Office ADA 49.
35. East Sussex Record Office ADA 159 p.18.
36. East Sussex Record Office SAS RF 5/7.

NOTES

37. East Sussex Record Office LAN 1.18.
38. History Of Lewes, Horsfield Vol. 1, p. 268.
39. East Sussex Record Office PAR 411/10/2-22.
40. East Sussex Record Office AMS 5745 87-94.
41. East Sussex Record Office AMS 5745 101-4.
42. Dunvan p. 368.
43. East Sussex Record Office WS 87.
44. Dunvan p. 369.
45. East Sussex Record Office AMS 5809.12.
46. Ibid., 13.
47. Ibid., 28.
48. Ibid., 18-31.
49. Victoria County History, Vol. 2, p. 104.
50. Field Archaeology Unit News No. 5, Winter 1996-7. I am grateful to Mr. Barber and the Field Archaeology Unit for a site plan.
51. East Sussex Record Office GLYNDE 2197.
52. Victoria County History, Vol. 7, p. 76, quoting Liber de Hyda (Rolls Series) 203.
53. Sussex Record Society, Vol. 34, p.5.
54. Close Roll 4 Chas 1.pt xxvii. No7.
55. British Library Add.Mss 39495.fo 401.
56. Victoria County History, Vol. 7, quoting Court of Wards Inq pm xxiv.202.
57. History Of Lewes, Horsfield, p.270.
58. Cal Anc Deeds A 14178.
59. *Sussex Notes and Queries,* Vol. 2, 145. *Sussex Record Society,* Vol. xiv 947, and *Sussex Record Society,* Vol. X, 169 & 283.
60. East Sussex Record Office ADA 45.
61. East Sussex Record Office LAN 309. This interesting map shows how Houndean had expanded into Ashcombe by the end of the eighteenth century.

Chapter 8

1. *Sussex Record Society,* Vol. 34, p. 17.
2. *Sussex Archaeological Collections,* Vol. 114, p. 51, quoting Elliott papers G1, p. 2 at Barbican House.

3. Dunvan, op. cit., p. 374.
4. Dunvan, op cit., p. 379.
5. *Sussex Record Society*, Vol. 38, p. 1. First charter of the Priory c.1089.
6. *The Hundred and the Hundred Rolls*, Merlin Press, 1930, pp. 280-2.
7. *Sussex Record Society*, Vol. 34, p. 193.
8. *Victoria County History* 7, p. 44, quoting Lay subsidies 190.
9. Lewes Priory Trust, 1997.
10. *Victoria County History* 7, p. 3.
11. Ibid., p. 44, quoting *Sussex Record Society*, Vol. 20, p. 412 and Court of Wards inq pm lxxi.59.
12. *Sussex Record Society*, Vol. 40.
13. British Library Add. Ch 30603-5.
14. L & P Hen VIII xvi.g.503(32) and CPRPM iv.p.188., quoted in *Sussex Archaeological Collections*, Vol. 114, p. 51.n.
15. *Sussex Notes & Queries*, Vol. 16 (#6), p. 196.
16. Dunvan, p. 407. Other sources also quote this.
17. East Sussex Records Office. Accession 1246.
18. *Sussex Archaeological Collections*, Vol. 58, p. 92, and *Recollections of a Sussex Parson*, Ellman p. 29.
19. *Sussex Notes & Queries*, Vol. 16 (#6), p. 194.
20. English Heritage Guide Book.
21. East Sussex Records Office, ADA 45.
22. *Sussex Archaeological Collections*, Vol. 46, p. 134-44.
23. *Place Names of Sussex*, Vol 2, p. 322, quoting Dugdale V.18.
24. Horsfield, *History of Lewes*, Vol. 1, but not in his later *History of Sussex*.
25. *Sussex Notes & Queries*, Vol. 16 (#6), p. 196.
26. Lower, *Worthies of Sussex*, Bacon, 1865, p. 193 n.
27. *Sussex Record Society*, Vol. 9.
28. Sussex Genealogical Centre, Hearth Tax Assessments, Paper 3. Mr Farrant agrees that my interpretation may be correct.
29. *Sussex Archaeological Collections*, Vol. 100, p. 77.
30. *Sussex Archaeological Collections*, Vol. 46. op. cit.
31. Sharpe Collection. *Sussex Archaeological Collections*, 209a, reproduced in *Sussex Churches*.
32. East Sussex Records Office, ADA 45 (1616).
33. Sussex Archaeological Trust. Business papers at Barbican House.

Appendix A

Domesday lists of tenants in chief holding lands in Lewes Rape (with Burgages in Lewes, where listed as held)
(The rents shown are for the total of the burgages)

Pre-conquest (with rent)	Burgages	Domesday Manor	Held By	Burgages Quitrent
Young Alnoth (fro King Edward)	7	Alciston	Abbot of St Martin, Battle	Not given
King Edward	11	Ditchling	W de Warenne	12s
" "	6	"	" " "	43d
Wilton Abbey	-	Falmer	Priory of St Pancras	-
Bishop of Chichester	3	Henfield	Bp. of Chichester	21d
Earl Godwin	-	Hurstpierpoint	Robert	-
Arch Bp. Canterbury	21	Malling	Arch.Bp.Canterbury	8s.8d
Queen Edith	26	Niworde	" " "	13s
Bishop of Chichester	3	Preston	Bp. of Chichester	18d
Earl Harold	26	Patcham	" " "	13s
" "	44	Rodmell	" " "	22s
St Peter's, Winchester	10	Southese	St Peters, Winchester	42d
Canons of Malling	7	Stanmer	Canons of Malling	21d

Mesne tenants of William De Warenne

Beeding lands	-	Aldrington	Godfrey	-
Wigot from King Edward	-	"	"	-
Wulfward	1	Allington	Ralph	6d
Edeva (Allodium)	4	"	Hugh	4s.0d
?	-	"	Nigel	-
Cola	-	Ashcombe	William son of Reginald	-
Bictric of E.Godwin	-	Brighton	Ralph	?
Freeholders (Allodium)	4	"	Widard	-
Wulfward	-	"	Wm. de Watteville	-
Falmer Villagers	-	Balmer	Gozo	8s.7d
A Falmer villager	-	"		-
Azor from Godwin	-	Barcombe	Wm. de Watteville	-
Villagers	18	Beeding	Hugh	-

UNKNOWN LEWES

Pre-conquest (with rent)	Burgages	Domesday Manor	Held By	Burgages Quitrent
Azor from King Edward	-	Benfield	Nigel	-
Thorgot	-	Benefield	Scotland	-
Leofwin	-	"	Alfred	-
Azor	2	Bevenden	Walter	18d
Frederick (Allodium)	1	Chiltington	Robert	12d
?	1½	"	A man at arms	8d
Godric	1	"	Godfrey	6d
Azor	9	Clayton	Wife of Wm. de Watteville	4s.7d
Harold	-	Fulking	Tesselin	-
Alnoth (Allodium)	4	Harpingden	Godfrey	20d
Wulfeva from King Edward	-	Hamsey	Ralph	-
Azor from King Edward	-	Hangleton	William de Watteville	-
Azor	7	Keymer	"	25d
Azor of K.Edward	-	Moulstone	Jocelyn	-
Alfheah (Allodium)	-	Newtimber	Ralph	-
E. Godwin	2	Orleswick	Nigel	10s
Alnoth (Allodium)	10	Ovingdean	Godfrey	5s
Cola of E.Godwin	-	Poynings	William son of Reginald	-
Leofhelm	2	Pangdean	W. de Warenne	2s
Osward (Allodium)	2	"	"	2s
Godwin from E. Godwin	9	Plumpton	Hugh son of Ranulph	4s.5d
Osward	-	Portslade	Osward	-
?	-	"	Albert	-
Leofnoth (Allodium)	3	Pavethorne	Leofnoth	18d
Osward	1½	Perching	Osward	9d
Belling from E. Godwin	½	"	Tesselin	2d
Azor of King Edward	-	"	William de Watteville	-
Heming from E. Godwin	-	Rottingdean	Hugh	-
Godwin (Priest)	1	Sadlescombe	Ralph	Not given
Leofwin	3	Streat	"	18d
4 freeholders (Allodium)	3	Warningore	Hugh	21d
Countess Gytha	1	Westmeston	Robert	nil
Alwin from Azor (Allodium)	¾	Wickham	Alwin from Wm. de Watteville	15d
Edeva	3	Winterbourne	Aldith	18d
Godric from King Edward	-	Wooton	Godfrey	-

172

Appendix B

Some named Officers of the barony or borough of Lewes.
The Steward was a personal servant of the lord of the manor and/or the barony. He was not a royal officer, as the reeve or sherrif was.

Date	Name	Role	Reference
1147-8	Adam the Sheriff	Sheriff	SRS40 p.25
c.1190	Sir Waryn deKyngestone (Steward of Earl Warenne)	Steward	SRS40 p.23 SRS40 p.21
	Robert	Porter (janitor)	Ibid. p.7
c.1215	Sir William de Moncell	Steward	SRS40 p.42
1240-1	William de Munceaus	Keeper	VCH7 p.20
1241-2	Peter de Savoy	"	"
1256-7	Hugh de Plumpton	Earl's sheriff	Cal Anc Dds
	Richard de Wiavill	Steward	" " " 4144
1265	Richard de la Vach	Steward	SRSXLIV p.6
1278	Oliver FitzEmis	Steward	VCH7 p.20
	Hamelin	Porter	"
1356-7	Thomas Hoo	Steward	SRS44
1378	(James Ferour John Peyntour)	Constables and townsmen	SNQXVII 2 p.49
1393-4	John North	Constable	AddCh.30556
1397	Thomas Podheye	King's weighing officer for wood	SAC91 pp.44-5
1398	Thomas Attacton	Porter	VCH7 p.20
1417	William Northampton	Bailiff	AddCh.30561
1428-9	William Chamber	"	PRO SC6 1474
1447-59	John Hanmere	"	AddCh. 30569
1465-6	Thomas Hoo [Verify]	Steward	SRS XLIV p.67
1471	Thomas Lancastre	Steward of Castle & borough	AddCh30569
1476-8	Thomas Lancastre	Bailiff of barony, and Castle & town of Lewes	DL29.7312.434
1476-8	Richard Luke	Constable	DL29.7312.434
1476-85	Henry Rabe or Rake	Porter	Cal Pat R No481
1498	Charies Barlow	"	SC6 1474
1499	Thomas Gaston	Constable	ESRO SASEG25

UNKNOWN LEWES

1499	Thomas Byrd	Constable	ESRO SASEG253
	Thomas Brian	Bailiff	AddCh 5701.fo48
1513-14	Thomas Michell	Receiver of the Duke of Norfolk	AddMss 5701.fo48
1524-5	Robert Batnour and Stephen Colyn	Bailiffs	AddCh30574&6
1526	Richard Frankwell and Thomas Audley	"	AddCh.30578
1528-30	Richard Ive	Bailiff	SC6 6305
1532-4	Nicholas Durrant	"	SC6 6158
1544	Clement Puggesley (First constable named in Town Book)	Constable	SRS 48
1551	John Battner Sr. and Richard Esterfield	Constables	AddCh 30589
1556	John Cotmot + illegible	Bailiffs	AddCh 30593
1568	John Ottringham	Constable	AddCh 30601-2
1569	John Young	Bailiff (barony/borough)	SPDom CaseA/6
1588-1616	Christopher Blaxton	Bailiff (for Lord Abergavenny)	ESRO DYK 1122
	Richard Marks (for Thos Sackville Lord Buckhurst)		
1594	Christopher Blaxton (for Lord Abergavenny)	Bailiff	ESRO DYK 1123

Appendix C

Crofts in Lewes

These crofts are the basic building blocks of many of the more recent properties in Lewes. This appendix is provided for those who may be interested in the origins of their land.

ALMONERS CROFT (or Garden) and other lands.
(Also, with others, called the Watermill Gardens, Southover.) Corner of Southover Road and Garden (once Gardener) Street. In All Saints and St Andrews. Cal Anc Deeds 30560. Bounded west Almoner's Garden, east meadow of John Bedeford, south, small watercourse and Mill of Watergate, north ditch of borough of Lewes. This is now part of the station car park.

AMERY LAND OR CROFT.
St Michael (Without the walls). Southwest end of Keere Street, approx sites of 59 grange road and 17 Keere Street. 1560 Land late of the Monastery of St Pancras called Amery (sic? Almonry) land in St Peter Westout and St Michael the Archangel, bounded west by a lane called Antioch Street and a croft called the Horsecroft, east by the highway from the Monastery of Lewes, and north by the tenement and garden late George Thornton. ESRO AMS 2705/2.

BUGATES.
Also known as Styles Field (All Saints). This two acre croft occupied the triangle of land between Church Twitten and Broomans Lane (other than the Church of All Saints and the cottage called 'Pinwell'), until Church Lane was diverted about 1705. It has been fully described in the main text. For a brief interval it was known as 'Styles Field' at the end of the seventeenth century. It has otherwise been known only by variations of the name of Bugates.

UNKNOWN LEWES

CASTLE BANKS.
Houndean Manor. St John sub Castro. 1787 Conveys to W. B. Langridge, waste on the north side of the Castle, part of the Castle Ditch *'Lately used by His Majesty's forces quartered at Lewes as an exercise ground or riding school, bounding to a certain high bank part of the Castle Bank belonging to William Bennett, granted from the waste 1789.'* (LAN 287 la.2r.3p) This is the site of the modern 55-65 New Road, waste land of the Manor of Houndean. (1825 ESRO ADA 165 p 34.)

CHURCH CROFT. Also Church Field. St Mary's & St Peter's.
Houndean Manor. Both sides of St Anne's Church Lane, St Mary's croft being now part of County Hall Car Park.

CONNYCROFT.
Houndean Manor. Mainly St Anne's but the bottom end may now be Southover. Lower south western end of Rotten Row lying west of Horsecroft qv 1615. SRS 34 p 5 John Saxpes (free tenant) held a copyhold croft called Connycroft from 1564-5 19 1/2 d.

DAPPS, OR DOPPS CROFT.
Houndean Manor. St John sub Castro. North of St John's Terrace. 1615 Henry Hider held a parcel of land called Dapps containing about 1/2 acre in the Parish of St John sub Castro in Lewes, paying 5d. This croft had been held by Dopp who lived at (modern) 614 High Street and held gardens behind. It is mainly the north side of Brack Mount and the north of Castle Banks.

DOBELL'S CROFT (not Dobell's Field q.v.)
Borough of Lewes. All Saints & St John sub Castro. c.1570 (KAO U269/E184) *'John Ottringham for a croft in St John sub Castro. 6s.'* The identification is reasonable but not certain. 1624 Walter Dobell. croft containing 3 acres late Lunsford's, Ottringham's, 6 shillings (SRS34). Within Little East Street, Green Wall, Wellington Street and North Street, in the parishes of All Saints and St John sub Castro, copyhold of Lewes Manor. Eventually the croft becomes a

APPENDIX C

property developers muddle. Comprises most of the land between North Street and Green Wall up to North Place, and the east end of East Street.

DOBELLS FIELD. Held of the Manor of Westmeston, in All Saints. On the north side of School Hill, now site of Albion Street. Dobell's field is not the same as Dobells Croft, and various conveyances confuse the two. 1625. *'W.Dobell dec'd was seized of the Manor of Westmeston alias Westminston, a mess. barn garden orchard & stable value £3 6s 8d and a croft cont'* 2 acres in Lewes 6s 8d. (qv. IPM 567 SRS29).

DOCKWISH.
Manor of Southover, outside the Borough. Water meadow south of the Winterbourne in 1362-3 (Cal Anc Deeds A4123). By 1383-4 it was granted to John Amblour of Lewes *'an enclosed meadow in Dokwyssch by the East Gate of Suthenovere adjoining a meadow belonging to the lands of Smithewicke and the Dyke of Watergate Mill.'* (CAD A4096, also mentioned in A 4123).

EARLS GARDEN.
Copyhold Manor of Lewes. Part All Saints, part St John Castro In 1447 was let to farm, to John Hanmer (PRO SC6 6158). It was later bounded by Abinger Place, Lancaster Street, North Street and West Street. This six acre croft was the largest piece of open space in Lewes. In 1594 it was spelt Earlsden, but by 1594 it was 'Earlsgarden', at a quit-rent of 18s 6d, (ESRO DYK 1123). It was later divided into three parts, the boundaries becoming St John's Street and Sun Street. The eastern part, between St John's Street and North Street became Townsend or Townsends Field, and the west part from Sun Street to Abinger Place became Woodcock Fields. The middle part presumably retained the name Earlsgarden. The present side street off St John's street named Earlsgarden was suggested by the writer, to preserve this early name.

FRIARS LAND.
Held of the Crown. All Saints south of Lower High Street The story of the Grey Friars is given in Chapter Five.

HORSECROFT.
Manor of Houndean. St Anne's Westout. South side of Rotten Row. First appears in 1503-4 (SRS34.p5), but by 1615 Thomas Ld. Buckhurst and Earl of Dorset held a parcel of land called Horsecroft alias Horescroft late Shermans in the parish of St Peter and Mary Westout in Lewes, paying 18d.

LONGES CROFT (later Matthews Croft).
Part Lewes part Clayton Manor. St John sub Castro. On the north side of Brack Mount, so named on Randoll's Map of 1620. Held in 1575 by Eleanor, widow of William Turle, occupied by Robert Long, then called the Earthe Croft or Castle Croft, bounded west by John Stempe's Croft, east and north by Lady Pelhams Croft. This land can be traced through to 1624 when John Matthew held 1/3 of Manor of Lewes, 2/3 of Manor of Clayton. 8d.

PAYNES WISH.
Southover Manor. Part within Southover, part All Saints. From opposite Watergate Lane to opposite Walwers Lane, between Southover Road and the Borough Boundary. Robert Lord Buckhurst held c.1558-9 by copyhold two acres of marsh land late Pankhurst once Malls, lying on the west side of the land of John Shurley called the Fryers, and on the north of his own lands paying 4 shillings. By 1787 it is a parcel of land called Payneswish. Parcel of the Manor of Southover containing 1 1/2 acres in St Michael and All Saints (ESRO BLE C2/29/4) *'... bounding to the bank or wall of the Town of Lewes. North the Mill Dyke south, lands formerly of Sir Thomas Pelham since of the Duke of Newcastle now of Henry Pelham ...'* called Fissenden's Garden. West, and land formerly Sir John Shirley [sic] now Apsley Pellatt east, lies between Lansdown Place & Pinwell Road.

APPENDIX C

RIDING HOUSE FIELD, (also HALLS CROFT, OR THE WOODCROFT).
Southover Manor. Part All Saints, part St John Castro. Bounded by Fisher Street, West Street, Market Street and Market Lane. 1425 Robert Smithwyk of Lewes to John Parker of Lewes. Garden in St John sub Castro and St Nicholas on the east side of 'Lodderslaan'. Thomas Pelham added in 1614 a barn & garden near Fisher Street in St John sub Castro, and a barn & garden of 1.r. in St John's (and the Woadcroft in St John & All Saints (30639).

THE PEPPERCORN.
Southover Manor, parish of Southover. VCH2. p. 412 quoting PCC 20 Fettiplace. 1511 Agnes Morley of Southover, by will to Roger Pugislee (a relative). *'The Pepir Come ... lying in the Parish of Southover ... at Watergate ...'* This land named as such then disappears, but is now the car park facing Southover Grange.

STAPLEY'S CROFT.
Manor of Lewes. All Saints. This croft first appears by this name in 1598, held of the Manor of Lewes Borough at a quit-rent of 3s 4d, but it was recorded as having had a previous owner. It was broken up for development at the end of the eighteenth Century. It measured three acres in 1699 (ESRO SAS C32). It took its name from the 1598 owner John Stapley (ESRO Aber I.fo.llv), who in addition owned (modern) 194-8 High Street, both areas of land passing from him by 1683 to Richard Isted, Gent. (ESRO ADA 49 3s 4d). The development covered the High Street frontage from 194-8, Market Street east side, part of North Street east side, and East Street (modern numbers 1-17)

STEWARDS INN CROFT.
This has been dealt with in Chapter Four.

ST JOHNS BROOKS.
Part All Saints, Part St John Castro, beside river, north from lower high street to the drove road by St John's church. In c.1506, Croyden

hath in farm a tenement (of Southerham Farm) and 18 acres of meadow 5 marks, 3s 4d.' (ESRO CP107 c.1506-27). This appears next as *'A brew house and 18 acres of marys (marsh?) land, against the freers in Lewes, wherein one Croyden dwelleth inne'* (WHG Mss at Barbican House, source not given.) For further information see The Town Brooks in St John sub Castro described in Chapter Four.

WESTOUT CROFT.
All Saints north of High Street (Schhol Hill). This is an interesting croft for its historical background, although it has proven impossible to trace. In 1535 it was held by Henry Squire (1536 Will ESRO A.la 26, died 1538), of the Manor of Westout at a rent of 2s 1d, containing *'about 3 acres by estimation'*.(ESRO AMS 5510/3). This probably became called Stapleys Croft (q.v.) although the process is not on record.

THE WOODCROFT.
In St John Castro & All Saints. Location not Established. Probably early name for Riding House Field q.v.. I have not been able to identify this croft, and I have to assume that 4 1/2 acres is an error (errors of this scale are found elsewhere in the town) and the true area corresponds to Riding House Field, confined within four roads as shown in the 1568 deed. In the circumstances, refer to Riding House Field.